1966

The Grateful Dead move into a communal house in the Haight-Ashbury district in San Francisco.

Owsley Stanley (also known as Bear) meets the band and briefly becomes their soundman. He would go on to design much of the Dead's iconic imagery, including the "stealie" — the lightning bolt through a skull — and the dancing bears.

1967

The Grateful Dead release their self-titled debut album.

Kreutzmann introduces Hart to the rest of the band, and he soon joins the lineup.

Police raid the Dead's house in Haight-Ashbury and find a stash of marijuana. Members of the band pay fines.

1968

The Grateful Dead briefly disbands when Pigpen and Weir are fired. Although both rejoin the band in short order, Constanten is added to play keys in place of Pigpen.

1969

New Riders of the Purple Sage make their debut. Garcia plays pedal steel for the band, which frequently opens for the Grateful Dead.

Garcia appears on the cover of *Rolling Stone*. He will appear on the cover 11 more times.

The Grateful Dead play a forgettable set at Woodstock in August and skip their set at Altamont in December, where Meredith Hunter is killed while the Rolling Stones perform.

... rleans, several members of the Grateful Dead are among 19 people arrested for drug possession.

Constanten leaves the band; Pigpen is briefly the only keyboard player.

Garcia first appears on stage with two of his most important non-Dead collaborators, Howard Wales and Merl Saunders.

Two classic Grateful Dead albums, *Workingman's Dead* and *American Beauty*, are released. "Uncle John's Band," "Casey Jones," "Friend of the Devil," "Sugar Magnolia," "Ripple" and "Truckin'" are among the songs on these two albums.

1971

Hart leaves the Grateful Dead; the main reason is that his dad, Leonard Hart, stole $70,000 from the band. Leonard Hart had been acting as the band's money manager.

Pigpen leaves the Grateful Dead for health reasons, although he will play with the band sporadically until the summer of 1972.

Keith Godchaux joins the band on keyboards; his wife, vocalist Donna Jean Godchaux, soon becomes a member as well.

1972

The Weir solo album *Ace* is released. The other members of the Grateful Dead play on the album, which contributes several concert staples, including "One More Saturday Night."

Timeline continued on page 96

STREET SIGN: BILL FEHR/SHUTTERSTOCK; MARIJUANA: YELLOWJ/SHUTTERSTOCK; GARCIA/HART: WIKI COMMONS; WOODSTOCK: WIKI COMMONS

D1597946

FRONT COVER PHOTOS: MarketOlya/Shutterstock, Reshetnyova Oxana/Shutterstock, Photoshot/Everett Collection, alevtina/Shutterstock
BACK COVER PHOTOS: : Eric Risberg/AP Photo, Peter Sanders/Rex Features/Everett Collection

Editor
Ben Nussbaum

Chief Content Officer
June Kikuchi

Managing Editor
Ethan Mizer

Art Director
Cindy Kassebaum

Multimedia Production Coordinator
Leah McGowan

i-5 publishing

Chief Executive Officer
Mark Harris

Chief Financial Officer
Nicole Fabian

Chief Sales Officer
Kim Huey-Steiner

Chief Marketing Officer
Beth Freeman Reynolds

Chief Digital Officer
Jennifer Black

Chief Technology Officer
Kartik Money

Chief Deadhead and Controller
Craig Wisda

Vice President, Direct Sales
Susan Roark

Book Division General Manager
Christopher Reggio

Marketing Director
Lisa MacDonald

Multimedia Production Director
Laurie Panaggio

Human Resources Director
Cherri Buchanan

Editorial, Production and Corporate Office
3 Burroughs, Irvine, CA 92618
949-855-8822

Grateful Dead is published by I-5 Publishing, LLC, 3 Burroughs, Irvine, CA 92618-2804. Corporate headquarters located at 3 Burroughs, Irvine, CA 92618. ©2015 by I-5 Publishing, LLC. All rights reserved. Reproduction of any material from this issue in whole or in part is strictly prohibited.

Registration No. R126851765

Printed in the U.S.A.

PETER SANDERS/REX USA/EVERETT COLLECTION

Dead

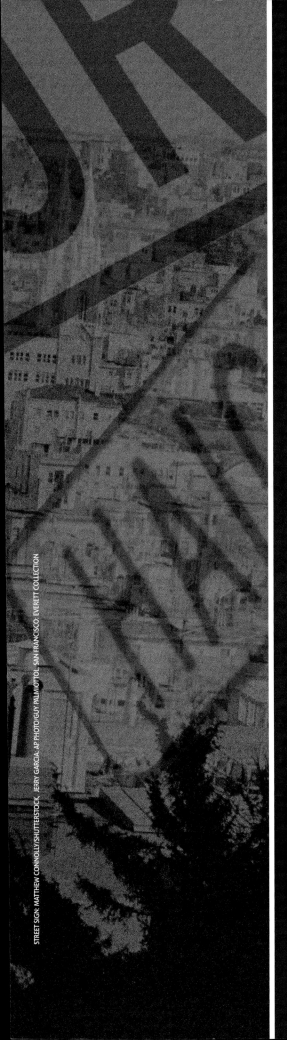

STREET SIGN: MATTHEW CONNOLLY/SHUTTERSTOCK; JERRY GARCIA: AP PHOTO/GUY PALUMBO; SAN FRANCISCO: EVERETT COLLECTION

the san francisco kid

The vision that drove the Grateful Dead was rooted in the mid-century Bay Area art scene.

BY PETER RICHARDSON

O f the countless bands that flashed across the American scene in the second half of the 20th century, why did the Grateful Dead achieve such durable success? Their status had almost nothing to do with commercial radio. Nor was the Dead's longevity due to their showmanship. Their live performances were their calling card, but they put almost no energy into the usual rock theatrics.

The Dead's countercultural image was certainly a factor. Hip, funny and smart, they seemed to create effortlessly and without artifice. For many, the Grateful Dead were cool because they gave mainstream American culture a wide berth and still managed to flourish. Wherever the Dead played, the Summer of Love lived on.

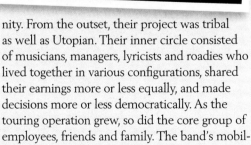

a novel
by Jack Kerouac

ON THE ROAD

American Ideals

The Grateful Dead's status as counterculture heroes masks an even more important source of their popularity. A large part of their appeal arose not from their resistance to American culture, but rather from their uncanny ability to tap into its inexhaustible Utopian energies. Living on the edge of novelty, inventing their own ways and means, the Dead pursued a singular, consistent and deeply idealistic vision.

Three Utopian urges were especially central to the Dead's project. First, they emphasized ecstasy — not the drug, but the feeling of transcendence. As Garcia explained in 1972, the Dead were "not for cranking out rock and roll, it's not for going out and doing concerts or any of that stuff, I think it's to get high … I'm not talking about unconscious or zonked out, I'm talking about being fully conscious."

Second, the Dead shared the American fascination with the open road. Garcia called the Dead's traveling culture his generation's "archetypal American adventure," the modern equivalent of joining the circus or riding freight trains.

Finally, the Dead were dedicated to commu-

nity. From the outset, their project was tribal as well as Utopian. Their inner circle consisted of musicians, managers, lyricists and roadies who lived together in various configurations, shared their earnings more or less equally, and made decisions more or less democratically. As the touring operation grew, so did the core group of employees, friends and family. The band's mobil-

Above: Ken Kesey and the Merry Pranksters' famous bus, named Furthur, appeared at Hempfest 2010 in Seattle, after recently being restored.

Right: Jack Kerouac's 1957 seminal novel, *On the Road*, fueled the Beat movement and generations of artists since.

TOP: JOE MABEL/WIKI COMMONS, BOTTOM: AP PHOTO

A Unique Scene

San Francisco in the 1950s was commercially connected but culturally isolated. Perhaps for this reason, the avant-garde played a different role in the city than it did elsewhere. According to Kenneth Rexroth, the grand old man of mid-century San Francisco letters, the city's underground arts scene was "dominant, almost all there is." Living on the nation's geographical and artistic margin, lacking established outlets for their work, San Francisco artists were constantly in the position of making their own party.

After World War II, writers of the San Francisco Renaissance offered different versions of an alternative, more connected and more fulfilling community. Their underlying impulses were a response to the violence and dislocation of the war, but much of their work also arose from a profound sense of insularity. As poet Gary Snyder put it later, "In the spiritual and political loneliness of America of the fifties, you'd hitch a thousand miles to meet a friend. … [In the] West coast of those days, San Francisco was the only city; and of San Francisco, North Beach."

Most of these writers had little or no financial support for their work. Meeting in bars or at informal dinner parties to talk politics, religion and art, they presented their work not as literary artifacts but as dramatic performances intended for (and sometimes aimed at) close friends. The interpersonal nature of their work helped create a sense of community that was otherwise lacking — not only in San Francisco, but in American mass society as well.

The San Francisco art community also reflected one aspect of the city's Gold Rush roots: a high tolerance for risk. If a painter decided to work on a single piece for six years, as Jay DeFeo did with "The Rose," so be it. And if she applied hundreds of pounds of paint over the years so that the work resembled a sculpture, even better. And if the paint underneath the new layers never quite dried, or if the piece fell apart when moved, or if the whole thing turned to goo when stored, those risks were worth taking. Fear of failure mattered less than the artist's commitment to her evolving vision.

The Beats Arrive

A new energy was added to the scene by the Beats, particularly Kerouac and his masterpiece *On the Road*, which featured cross-country car trips and spirited adventures. His fictional

The Trieste Cafe, located on upper Grant Avenue in San Francisco circa 1969. The North Beach district, of which the cafe was a part, served as the epicenter of the Beat movement.

ity didn't impede their efforts to create community. Band member Mickey Hart told one writer, "We went out there and got this army in tow."

If these ideals help explain the band's success, where did they originate? Here the conventional wisdom refers us to that grand abstraction, the '60s. Once upon a time, teenagers had sex, used drugs and listened to loud music.

This is certainly true as far as it goes, but conventional wisdom fails to account for the Grateful Dead's remarkable staying power. Yes, the Dead were the quintessential '60s phenomenon, but they were also America's most popular touring band more than two decades after Woodstock.

Focusing on the '60s also obscures important aspects of the band's prehistory. In many ways, the main features of the Dead's project were formed by 1958. This was Jerry Garcia's miracle year, when he was 15 and 16. He received his first guitar, smoked his first joint, took courses at the California School of Fine Arts and read Jack Kerouac's *On the Road*. None of these experiences was especially unusual, but when we set them against the larger cultural forces that were sweeping through the San Francisco Bay Area at the time, and when we consider the profound effect they had on Jerome John Garcia, they help us understand the Dead's Utopian impulses and the band's sustained appeal.

AP PHOTO

Jack Kerouac, the visionary author of *On the Road*, challenged mainstream assumptions and earned a place as one of the seminal voices of the Beat movement.

odyssey glorified spontaneous, intense experiences, often fueled by drugs. Bebop jazz, with its soaring improvisations, provided the Beat soundtrack, and Kerouac consciously adapted its methods to his own writing. The narrator's name, Sal Paradise, signals the novel's Utopian theme, and he reinforces it early on: "I was a young writer and I wanted to take off. Somewhere along the line I knew there'd be girls, visions, everything; somewhere along the line the pearl would be handed to me."

The novel's hero was based on Neal Cassady, whose energy and thirst for experience represented a romantic frontier ideal. In real life, cross-country road trips bonded Kerouac and Cassady and prompted a compositional style that captured the spirit of their journeys. After extensive planning and outlining, Kerouac banged out the manuscript for *On the Road* in a series of Benzedrine-fueled raptures.

On the Road challenged mainstream American values in several ways. Its key relationships aren't found in nuclear families, but rather in male friendships forged through shared adventures. In their Bohemian exuberance, the characters decline almost everything Main Street might recognize as worthy: sobriety, common sense, hard work, monogamy, conventional religion and patriotism. Although Sal realizes that his paradise lacks something, that his frantic questing masks a conceptual emptiness, he sets aside his misgivings when the next adventure

Beatnik poet Bill Margolis posts one of his poems to the wall of a bagel shop in San Francisco in 1959.

PHOTOS: AP PHOTO

beckons. "We were all delighted," Sal says, "we all realized we were leaving confusion and nonsense behind and performing our one and noble function of the time, *move*."

Garcia Gets Plugged In

Reading *On the Road* changed Jerry Garcia's life, but he discovered it only by pursuing another artistic interest. Bored at school, he mostly focused on his Danelectro guitar, which he received for his 15th birthday, and marijuana, which he later said was right up his alley. But Garcia was also a capable illustrator, and he enrolled in a weekend program at the California School of Fine Arts (now the San Francisco Art Institute). Garcia's mentor there was Wally Hedrick, whose example appealed directly to a teenager looking for more. Garcia later said that he learned from Hedrick that "art is not only something you do, but something you are as well."

That lesson opened up a world of new possibilities — not only in terms of making art, but also in how to live like an artist. Hedrick and his artist wife, Jay DeFeo, lived up the hill from the Fillmore Auditorium. Their neighbors included poets Michael and Joanna McClure and Dave Getz, who studied painting at CSFA and later played drums for both Big Brother & the Holding Company and Country Joe & the Fish.

CSFA faculty member Carlos Villa stressed the importance of their home for visiting artists. "Wally and Jay's house on Fillmore was the unofficial first stop on any art itinerary — anyone important in the art world — national or international — theirs was the first stop," he recalled. It was there that DeFeo worked steadily on "The Rose," her epic painting, which took up an entire wall of the flat.

CSFA parties could be wild. Laird Grant, Garcia's boyhood friend, later recalled a Halloween shindig when they were teenagers: "This big limo pulled up in front of the California School of Fine Arts. This chick got out in this fur coat and left it there. She was totally stark naked with a raisin in her navel. She came as a cookie. … To her, it was nothing at all. But in '56 or '57, it was quite unusual."

Many CSFA artists were also taking drugs to heighten their perceptions. A 1957 issue of *Semina*, an underground journal connected to CSFA and published by artist Wallace Berman, included two photographs of poet Philip Lamantia injecting heroin. Another issue was

originally titled *Cannabis Sativa*. While visiting Michael McClure in 1958, Berman described the Native American uses of peyote and left behind some buttons in McClure's apartment. McClure ingested them and wrote a poem about the experience for the journal.

Never expecting to make money from their art, Hedrick and his colleagues worked without concern for posterity or publicity. "We knew that we weren't going to be able to show our own work," Hedrick told the Smithsonian Institution later, "and so the answer was to start our own gallery." In 1954, Hedrick helped organize the Six Gallery, which hosted the first public reading of Allen Ginsberg's "Howl" in 1955. It was a signal event in Beat history. Kerouac drank from a bottle of Burgundy and scatted during Ginsberg's performance.

It was Hedrick who introduced Garcia to Kerouac, *On the Road* and Beat culture more generally. Garcia cited the novel's formative power: "A germinal moment for me was back when I was in high school going to the San Francisco Art Institute [CSFA] on weekends, just when the words 'Beat generation' began hitting the papers. We asked my teacher, Wally Hedrick, about the phrase, and he said, 'Well, there's this book, *On the Road*, and it's all in there.' I was an impressionable San Franciscan,

Jack Kerouac originally wrote *On the Road* on a single, 119-foot-long semi-translucent piece of paper.

AP PHOTO

PHOTOSHOT/EVERETT COLLECTION

The Dead were heavily influenced by the revolutionary art and seismic cultural shifts initiated by the Beats.

really taken with the North Beach scene, and this stuff began to surface."

For Garcia, much of the novel's appeal lay in its musicality and in its romantic depiction of travel. "Then in the next couple of years I read Kerouac, and I recall in '59 hanging out with a friend who had a Kerouac record, and I remember being impressed — I'd read this stuff, but I hadn't heard it, the cadences, the flow, the kind of endlessness of the prose, the way it just poured off," he said. "It was really stunning to me. His way of perceiving music — the way he wrote about music and America — and the road, the romance of the American highway, it struck me. It struck a primal chord. It felt familiar, something I wanted to join in. It wasn't like a club; it was a way of seeing."

Reading *On the Road* was so influential that

the adult Garcia had difficulty distinguishing his artistic identity from Kerouac's influence. "It became so much a part of me that it's hard to measure; I can't separate who I am now from what I got from Kerouac," he said. "I don't know if I would ever have had the courage or the vision to do something outside with my life — or even suspected the possibilities existed — if it weren't for Kerouac opening those doors."

A Vision

Garcia's encounter with the mid-century art scene furnished him with the core principles for his lifelong project. "I wanted to do something that fit in with the art institute, that kind of self-conscious art — 'art' as opposed to 'popular culture,'" he recalled much later. Well before Garcia qualified for a California driver's license, he was absorbing a rich and historically specific set of ideas about what it was to be an artist. The 1960s in general, and LSD in particular, fueled that conception, but much of it was summed up by a small sign that mid-century artist Jess Collins posted in his San Francisco studio.

THE SEVEN DEADLY VIRTUES OF CONTEMPORARY ART:

Originality
Spontaneity
Simplicity
Intensity
Immediacy
Impenetrability
Shock

The Grateful Dead absorbed these deadly virtues and reflected them in their music. By the mid-'90s, the Dead were a long way away from the insular, Bohemian art community that Garcia stumbled upon in 1958, but they still lived and made music according to their original precepts.

The Dead were nothing if not collaborative, and their achievement far outstripped the contributions of any individual member. They frequently compared their experience to Theodore Sturgeon's *More Than Human*, the 1953 science fiction novel whose protagonist is comprised of several beings who act as a single organism and thereby overcome their individual deficiencies. But it's also true that the band looked to Garcia for direction, and lyricist Robert Hunter described their organization as a reflection of Garcia's mind.

What, then, preoccupied that mind? First and foremost, a vision of what it was to be an artist, a vision shaped by his early contact with the painters and writers of the San Francisco Renaissance. Garcia saw his teachers — broadly defined to include Kerouac — making art, improvising, taking risks, getting high, defying the square world, exploring weirdness, downplaying commerce and radiating irreverence. By emphasizing the Utopian ideals of ecstasy, mobility and community, these teachers offered Garcia an artistic framework that was enticing, flexible and durable — so durable, in fact, that Garcia and the Grateful Dead never deviated significantly from it. ●

Allen Ginsberg's poetry helped ignite the Beat movement.

AP PHOTO

BEATLES: MIRRORPIX/EVERETT COLLECTION; DEAD: AP PHOTO; STONES: RETNA/PHOTOSHOT/EVERETT COLLECTION

THE DEAD, THE STONES & THE BEATLES

Three iconic bands intersected and overlapped throughout their musical histories.

BY PETER SMITH AND IAN INGLIS

On the heels of the British Invasion of 1964 that reshaped American popular music, almost every band in the U.S. in the mid-1960s was influenced by the Beatles and the Rolling Stones. The Grateful Dead were no exception.

In the band's early years, the Stones exerted the greatest influence. "In the '65 to '66 period, they just basically wanted to be the Rolling Stones," according to Bill Kreutzmann's son, Justin, who has directed two documentaries about the Dead. "They just wanted to make blues records like the Rolling Stones." And it wasn't only the Stones' music that struck a chord with the Dead. The ramshackle look pioneered by the Stones fit the Dead's image much better than the widely copied Beatles' look: It's hard to imagine Pigpen sporting a moptop or the entire band decked out in suits!

WHITEHAVEN/SHUTTERSTOCK

The Beatles were an inescapable influence, too: All the band members saw *A Hard Day's Night* and, according to Bob Weir, the impact was immediate. "The Beatles were why we turned from a jug band into a rock 'n' roll band," Weir said.

For Jerry Garcia, the Beatles' significance went beyond music. "They were real important to everybody," Garcia said. "It was like saying, 'You can be young, you can be far out and you can still make it.' They were making people happy. That happy thing — that's the stuff that counts — something that we could all see right away."

The Stones: All Down the Line

"For me, the most resonant thing was hearing the Rolling Stones play music that I'd grown up with, the Chess [Records] stuff," Garcia said. "That was surprising because it was music that had already happened in my life, and then hearing it again was like, 'Right, that would be fun to play.' In the Grateful Dead's earliest version as a bar band, the option was to play Beatles stuff or Rolling Stones, and we always opted for whatever the Stones were doing."

"We had learned a lot from listening to the Rolling Stones, going so far as to cover some of their covers," band member Phil Lesh said.

It's hardly surprising that the 1965-66 War-locks/Grateful Dead repertoire included many songs performed or recorded by the Stones: "Promised Land," "Johnny B. Goode," "Around and Around," "Not Fade Away," "Hi-Heel Sneakers," "Pain in My Heart," "I Just Want to Make Love to You," "King Bee," "Little Red Rooster," "Walkin' the Dog" and "It's All Over Now."

The Dead broke new ground in 1966 by covering an original Stones song, "Empty Heart," credited to Nanker Phelge, a collective pseudonym used by the Stones in their early years (the Dead similarly employed the name McGannahan Skjellyfetti for group compositions). This rarity surfaced on the 2005 *Rare Cuts and Oddities* CD. The Dead went on to perform several other Jagger-Richards compositions, including "The Last Time," with 70 performances from 1990-95, and "Satisfaction," with 31 performances from 1980-94.

Although the live versions of Stones' compositions were never concert mainstays, the Dead's versions of songs also covered by the Stones were revisited again and again. Three maintained their position in the band's stage repertoire all the way to 1995 — over the Dead's 30-year career, "Not

The Rolling Stones, (from left) Brian Jones, Bill Wyman, Charlie Watts, Keith Richards and Mick Jagger, in the early 1960s

Mick Jagger and Keith Richards in concert in 1976, at Leicester Granby Hall

LEFT: DEZO HOFFMANN/REX USA/EVERETT COLLECTION. RIGHT: GRAHAM WILTSHIRE/REX USA/EVERETT COLLECTION

The Grateful Dead in the early 1970s

"A Heavy Trip"

The Monterey International Pop Festival in June 1967 featured the Dead as performers, the Rolling Stones' Brian Jones as visitor/occasional announcer, and Paul McCartney and Mick Jagger as (non-attending) festival advisers. A more substantial connection followed in December 1969, when the Dead and the Stones both agreed to appear at a free concert to be held at the Altamont Speedway just outside of San Francisco. Dead manager Rock Scully's idea to bring together what he described as "the two most delusional and drug-drenched bands on the planet" became increasingly attractive to the Stones after they were heavily criticized over the extortionate pricing of their 1969 U.S. tour tickets.

Scully's recommendation to use Hell's Angels as security on the evening of the Altamont concert rapidly backfired. As violence and frustration among the 300,000 spectators mounted, the Dead quickly assessed the situation and left the site, leaving the Stones alone to become historically and irrevocably linked with the ensuing chaos and the death of Meredith Hunter, stabbed just feet from the stage. (Read more about Altamont in "Festival Days & Nights" on page 20.)

Fade Away," "Around and Around" and "Little Red Rooster" were performed onstage 531, 418 and 272 times, respectively.

The Beatles: From Me to You

The Dead's early and extensive borrowing from the Stones' musical catalogue wasn't repeated with Beatles music. All three bands shared a common admiration for Chuck Berry, but while blues and rhythm 'n' blues were key influences for both the Dead and the Stones, the Beatles also drew much of their early inspiration from American rock 'n' roll, country, soul and Brill Building pop.

Apart from two infamously chaotic Pigpen-led renditions in 1969 of "Hey Jude," the band's relationship with the music of the Beatles didn't begin in earnest until the 1980s, when the Dead used the "Hey Jude" na-na-na-na chorus 28 times between 1985 and 1990, segueing out of their version of Traffic's "Dear Mr. Fantasy." In the same decade, the Dead sometimes performed other Beatles songs, notably "Revolution" (1983-90) and "Why Don't We Do It in the Road" (1984-86).

In the 1990s, the Dead began to feature songs from the Beatles' psychedelic period: Lennon-McCartney's "Lucy in the Sky With Diamonds" with 19 performances from 1993-95, "Rain" with 12 performances from 1992-95, and "Tomorrow Never Knows" with 12 performances from 1992-95 (segueing out of The Who's "Baba O'Reilly"), as well as George Harrison's "I Want To Tell You" with seven

PETER SANDERS/REX USA/ EVERETT COLLECTION

The Beatles' early clean-cut, mop-top look was frequently emulated and stood in contrast to the Dead's more laid back West Coast vibe.

EVERETT COLLECTION

performances from 1994-95 and "It's All Too Much" with six performances in 1995. The reason for this upsurge of Beatles songs during the 1990s isn't clear, although it's likely that Lesh's longstanding campaign to include more Beatles' material was boosted by the arrival in 1990 of keyboardist Vince Welnick, who sang lead vocals on two of the songs and is rumored to have led the band through a soundcheck rehearsal of "Paperback Writer."

The Bands Play On

The members of the Dead played in a bewildering variety of side projects, many of which dipped into either the Stones' or the Beatles' songbooks. Garcia's bluegrass-based band Old and in the Way performed the Stones' "Wild Horses" on many occasions. The various bands that Weir has led, both before and after Garcia's death, have always used a sprinkling of Lennon-McCartney (and Harrison) and Jagger-Richards material.

Lesh, with his constantly changing cast of bandmates, has been the most prolific performer of the other bands' best material: At last count, Phil Lesh and Friends have covered 33 Beatles' and 23 Stones' songs.

Perhaps the most celebrated instance of Lesh and Weir showing their affection for the Beatles occurred during Furthur's 2011 spring tour. The band played the entire *Abbey Road* album, initially playing one song per night (in the correct

order!), culminating on Lesh's 71st birthday with a note-perfect rendition of the album's concluding suite of songs.

Come Together?

By the time the Dead's first album was released in 1967, both British bands had long since abandoned cover versions and were concentrating exclusively on their own compositions.

Nevertheless, given that, individually and collectively, the Beatles, the Stones and the Dead actively pursued musical partnerships with other contemporary musicians, it's surprising that there have been no (known) musical collaborations between members of the Dead and the other bands. However, the separate orbits each band followed did occasionally collide to bring them into direct or indirect contact — often with momentous results.

In April 1967, shortly after the photo shoot for the cover of *Sgt. Pepper's Lonely Hearts Club Band*, Paul McCartney flew to San Francisco to check out the psychedelic scene. With Jefferson Airplane's Marty Balin acting as his guide, he picked up on many of the ideas and events that had helped define the emergent counterculture — including, crucially, the coast-to-coast bus trip undertaken in 1964 by Ken Kesey and the Merry Pranksters, with whom the Dead had a close association.

On the flight back to Britain with Beatles' roadie Mal Evans, McCartney began to combine

Imagine "Imagine"

In 1972, Garcia guested on Merl Saunders' *Heavy Turbulence* **album, which included a version of John Lennon's "Imagine." When Lennon subsequently attended a Jerry Garcia Band show in New York City, he accepted Garcia's invitation to join him on stage the following night, promising to return the next day to "work up a few tunes." Sadly, he failed to return, and the opportunity to see and hear the leaders of Britain's and America's two most revered and influential bands was lost.**

his fascination with what he had seen in San Francisco with his own childhood memories of trips to the seaside. The result, shown on U.K. TV screens several months later, was the hour-long *Magical Mystery Tour.*

Shortly before Garcia's death in August 1995, McCartney and his wife Linda Eastman unearthed four rolls of black-and-white photographs of the Dead taken by Linda in 1967. The photos were so numerous that McCartney was able to edit them into a nine-minute movie: *Grateful Dead: A Photofilm.* The film premiered in London in October 1996.

McCartney had been in correspondence with Garcia about the project up to the time of his death, and explained, "He was a painter and I thought he'd like this. ... I suppose it has become a little bit of a tribute to Jerry." When asked about the Grateful Dead's versions of Beatles' songs, he replied, "I was aware that they did some of our stuff, several of our songs, and took it as a great compliment." ●

Above: Mick Jagger and the Stones had a style the Dead could identify with.

Left: Members of the Stones and Beatles collaborated for the 1968 TV special *The Rolling Stones Rock & Roll Circus.* From left, Eric Clapton, John Lennon, Mitch Mitchell and Keith Richards.

TOP: MIRRORPIX/EVERETT COLLECTION, RIGHT: EVERETT COLLECTION

The Other

Anthem of the Sun
1968

SONG WRITTEN BY: Bob Weir and Bill Kreutzmann

VOCAL: Bob Weir

PERFORMED 604 TIMES. One of the most played songs in the Dead's history, it was played continuously from 1967 to 1995, with no long breaks aside from the Dead's '75-'76 hiatus. Frequently played after a drum solo, the song was the main second-set jam centerpiece in many shows. Prior to 1971, it was played as part of a suite with Garcia's "Cryptical Envelopment," which briefly reappeared for five performances in the summer of 1985.

FIRST PERFORMED: Oct. 22, 1967, at the Winterland Arena in San Francisco

LAST PERFORMED: July 8, 1995, at Soldier Field in Chicago

KEY LYRIC: "The bus came by and I got on. That's when it all

According to Bob Weir, "The Other One" is "one of the first tunes I ever wrote." It was his first original song on a Dead album.

. . . .

This tune marked the first appearance of a rose in a Dead song. Roses would become a common symbol in Dead imagery.

. . . .

On *Anthem of the Sun*, the "Other One" suite was divided into tracks with whimsical titles. According to Weir, "The names of the songs on the first part of side one were all just made up for publishing purposes. Otherwise we only would have gotten publishing money for one song."

. . . .

A number of guests played in "The Other One" over the years, including David Crosby, John Cipollina, Clarence Clemons, Branford Marsalis, Steve Miller, Santana and Ornette Coleman.

Jerry Garcia:

"It's wide open and it's got a great drive to it, those triplets. It's one of those things that you can still take anywhere. There's no way for it to get old. I don't relate to the lyrics, exactly; I relate to the way it sounds. And it sounds modern."

WEIR: MORRY GASH/AP PHOTO. GARCIA: NORTHPHOTO/SHUTTERSTOCK

One

Mickey Hart:

"The thing about 'The Other One' that was so thrilling was that it had all these climaxes at this incredible rate — and it was already at a very strong pace. … It was totally spontaneous, but the idea was to go out."

THE BUS TO NEVER-EVER LAND

"Cowboy Neal at the wheel of a bus to never-ever land" refers to Neal Cassady, who was the inspiration for the central hero of Jack Kerouac's *On the Road*. After Cassady gained notoriety through the book, he spent time as the driver of the Merry Pranksters' bus and hung out with the Dead during the Acid Trips and afterwards. "There's no experience in my life yet that equals riding with Cassady," Garcia said.

· ·

Cassady died in Mexico on Feb. 4, 1968. Weir claims that he unknowingly wrote the verse about Cassady that very day, while the Dead were on tour: "One night it sort of came to me. … I wrote the verses, and we played the gig that night and came home the next day, and when we came home we learned the news that Neal had died that night." But the story isn't quite true, since Weir had written the verse for Neal back in November '67.

BUSTED FOR A BALLOON

"The heat came round and busted me for smiling on a cloudy day" refers to an incident where Bob Weir threw a water balloon at a policeman. "The cops used to harass us every chance they got. They didn't care for the hippies back then. … I got him right square on the head, and he couldn't tell where it was coming from, but then I had to go downstairs and walk down the street and just grin at him, and sorta rub it in a little bit. … He didn't have a thing on me … but I did get thrown in jail."

HART: WIKI COMMONS, BALLOONS: UAWOLF0180/SHUTTERSTOCK

FESTIVAL DAYS & NIGHTS

The Grateful Dead played at some of the biggest parties in the golden age of rock 'n' roll.

BY GILLIAN GAAR

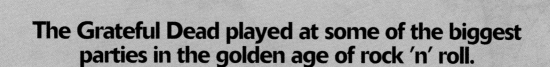

Large outdoor concerts are a standard part of summer now, but they only became a rock 'n' roll fixture in the late 1960s, when the biggest bands on the planet gathered together for festivals that are still legendary. The Grateful Dead had their turn on stage at some of the most notable festivals in music history, but the band's sets were mostly characterized by odd circumstances.

The Monterey International Pop Music Festival, June 16-18, 1967

Monterey Pop began when record producer Alan Pariser and promoter Ben Shapiro arranged for folk-rock group the Mamas and the Papas to headline a one-day music festival at the Monterey Fairgrounds in Monterey, Calif. (the same venue used for the Monterey Jazz Festival and the Monterey Blues Festival) in early 1967. The event was to become the first major rock music festival and the template for later iconic festivals, including Woodstock in 1969.

Then, as the group's producer, Lou Adler, recalled in the book *A Perfect Haze*, a night of indulging in what Adler euphemistically referred to as "California dreamin'" gave Adler and the Mamas and Papas' lead singer John Phillips the idea to make the show a charity endeavor, with proceeds benefiting various music-related causes. Shapiro had wanted to make money on the venture and bowed out, but Adler and Phillips ran with the idea, fundraising and setting up a board of governors for the event. Pariser was on the board of governors and remained a co-producer.

AP PHOTO

At the Monterey International Pop Music Festival, the Grateful Dead played between The Who (lead singer Roger Daltrey is pictured above) and Jimi Hendrix (left).

The Jimi Hendrix Experience

Monterey Pop Set List

1. "Killing Floor"
2. "Foxy Lady"
3. "Like a Rolling Stone"
4. "Rock Me Baby"
5. "Hey Joe"
6. "Can You See Me"
7. "The Wind Cries Mary"
8. "Purple Haze"
9. "Wild Thing"

The dates were set for June 16-18, and it was already May, but the festival came together quickly. The producers wanted the festival to represent "all genres of the immediate past, the present and the future of contemporary music," and the festival brought together musicians from major cities around the country, England and even as far away as India with the inclusion of renowned sitarist Ravi Shankar.

Because the festival was an L.A.-organized event, San Francisco musicians were initially reluctant to sign on. There was a rivalry between the two cities, with artists and fans from both believing that they had the more authentic rock scene. But *San Francisco Chronicle* journalist Ralph Gleason liked the idea of the festival, and he set up meetings between festival producers and the managers of prominent Bay Area bands, including the Grateful Dead.

The Dead's co-managers, Rock Scully and Danny Rifkin, looked out for the band's interests at the event. "Rifkin … pepper[ed] Adler with concerns about logistics, ticketing, staging and

PHOTOS: BRUCE FLEMING/AP IMAGES

Drummer Keith Moon of The Who performs during the Monterey International Pop Musical Festival.

BRUCE FLEMMING/AP IMAGES; BACKGROUND: EVERETT COLLECTION

The Who
Monterey Pop Set List

1. "Substitute"
2. "Summertime Blues"
3. "Pictures of Lily"
4. "A Quick One, While He's Away"
5. "Happy Jack"
6. "My Generation"

profits generated from the festival," co-authors Harvey and Kenneth Kubernik note in *A Perfect Haze*. When Rifkin learned the concerts were to be filmed, he threatened to pull the Dead off the bill and stage a free "anti-festival" in protest. The festival's spirit of "Music, Love, Flowers" won him over, but his resistance to letting the Dead become involved meant that the cameras were not turned on when the Dead performed.

It was nonetheless a coup for the Dead to be involved in the event. The band's self-titled first album had come out in March 1967. The festival attracted a lot of media attention and the exposure certainly helped boost the band's profile. The organizers were anxious for everything to run smoothly. They met with Monterey's mayor and police chief to ensure the locals wouldn't become too ruffled by the sudden invasion of that new creature, the hippie. The effort paid off: There were no generational clashes during the weekend.

The first group to step on the stage when the festival kicked off on June 16 was L.A. pop band the Association. By the time the Dead made their appearance on Sunday, June 18, audiences had been treated to sets by the Animals, Simon and Garfunkel, Janis Joplin, the Byrds, Laura Nyro and Otis Redding, among others. The Dead were given an unenviable slot, stuck between The Who and Jimi Hendrix, highenergy acts that were determined to outdo each other. The Who threw down the gauntlet first, smashing instruments at the end of "My Generation," shocking audience members who were more attuned to the peace and love aspects of the event.

SHANKAR: BRUCE FLEMING/REX FEATURES/EVERETT COLLECTION BAEZ: EVERETT COLLECTION

Ravi Shankar
Monterey Pop Set List

1. "Rāga Bhimpalasi"
2. "Rāga Todi-Rupak Tal" (7 Beats)
3. "Tabla Solo In Ektal" (12 Beats)
4. "Rāga Shuddha Sarang-Tintal" (16 Beats)
5. "Dhun In dadra and fast teental" (6 and 16 beats)

The Dead were unruffled by the challenge, playing a four-song set of "Cold Rain and Snow," "Viola Lee Blues," "Alligator" and "Caution (Do Not Stop on Tracks)." The band tried to generate a bit of energy by urging the audience to get up and dance, only to be thwarted by the ushers, who kept people in their seats and off of the stage.

The set's momentum was further interrupted when Peter Tork of the Monkees was sent on stage to try and curtail the gatecrashers who were trying to break into the festival in the mistaken belief that the Beatles were there. "This is the last concert," bassist Phil Lesh said with some exasperation. "Why not let them in anyway?" The two men bantered for a few minutes as Lesh continued to needle Tork. "The Beatles aren't here, come in anyway!" said Lesh. "If the Beatles were here they'd probably want you to come." As the crowd cheered Lesh on, Tork finally left the stage.

The band was "much enlivened" for the rest of the performance, according to critic Robert Christgau: "By the end of the set [Bob] Weir and Jerry Garcia were riffing back and forth in the best guitar-playing of the Festival."

Though the band wouldn't appear on the various live albums from the festival or in D.A. Pennebaker's documentary *Monterey Pop*, they were name-checked in the Animals' song about the event, "Monterey," which includes the lyric, "The Grateful Dead blew everybody's mind."

The Woodstock Music & Art Fair, Aug. 15-17, 1969

Woodstock was the quintessential '60s festival. Over 400,000 people were drawn to Max Yasgur's farm just outside of Bethel, N.Y., to experience "3 days of peace & music." The Grateful Dead were one of 32 acts that performed at the event, alongside Joan Baez, Sly and the Family Stone, Joe Cocker, Tim Hardin and The Band, among others.

The festival came together when promoter Michael Lang (who had produced the Miami Pop Festival in 1968) and his friend, Capitol Records exec Artie Kornfeld, hooked up with John Rob-

Sly & The Family Stone

Woodstock Set List

1. "M'Lady"
2. "Sing A Simple Song"
3. "You Can Make It If You Try"
4. "Everyday People"
5. "Dance To The Music"
6. "Music Lover"
7. "Want To Take You Higher"
8. "Love City"
9. "Stand!"

EVERETT COLLECTION; BACKGROUND: EVERETT COLLECTION

erts and Joel Rosenman, two young businessmen who had taken out ads in major newspapers saying they were looking for investment opportunities. The four men decided to produce a festival and formed the company Woodstock Ventures, choosing the name because they planned to stage their event in Woodstock, N.Y.

It turned out that the company was prematurely named; once residents of the small town, just over 100 miles north of New York City,

Joan Baez

Woodstock Set List

1. "Oh Happy Day"
2. "The Last Thing On My Mind"
3. "I Shall Be Released"
4. Story about how the Federal Marshalls came to take David Harris into custody
5. "No Expectations"
6. "Joe Hill"
7. "Sweet Sir Galahad"
8. "Hickory Wind"
9. "Drug Store Truck Driving Man"
10. "I Live One Day at a Time"
11. "Take Me Back to the Sweet Sunny South"
12. "Let Me Wrap You in My Warm and Tender Love"
13. "Swing Low, Sweet Chariot"
14. "We Shall Overcome"

got wind of the festival, they hastily refused permission. Locations in Saugerties and Wallkill were considered, but the organizers were again met with opposition.

Finally, Lang was introduced to Yasgur, who ran a dairy farm in Bethel, 60 miles south of Woodstock, and he agreed to make his property available for the event. Not every resident in Bethel was happy about it — one disgruntled citizen posted a sign reading "Stop Max's Hippie Music Festival. No 150,000 hippies here. Buy no milk." — but the organizers garnered enough support for the festival to proceed.

Advance ticket sales were good, and the organizers expected around 200,000 people to attend. What they weren't expecting was that thousands more without tickets would also try to attend. People began arriving before the festival started, and it didn't take long for the freeway to become snarled in a miles-long traffic jam, which was only made worse when some drivers abandoned their cars and walked to the festival. Arriving at the site without a ticket didn't present any problems for attendees, as skimpy fencing wasn't much of an obstacle. As a result, the farm was flooded with 200,000 paying guests and at least as many more who didn't pay a cent.

Despite rain, plus the lack of sufficient food, shelter and proper sanitation, the festival proceeded relatively smoothly. Jimi Hendrix's performance of "The Star-Spangled Banner" would become iconic, and the artist Melanie would have a top 40 hit with her song about the event, "Lay Down (Candles in the Rain)." But the Dead, who performed on Aug. 16, after Mountain and before Creedence Clearwater

Revival, didn't feel they rose to the occasion.

"We played such a bad set at Woodstock," Jerry Garcia later told *Jazz & Pop* magazine. "The weekend was great, but our set was terrible. We were all pretty smashed, and it was at night. Like we knew there were a half-million people out there, but we couldn't see one of them. There were about a hundred people on stage with us, and everyone was scared that it was gonna collapse. On top of that, it was raining or wet, so that every time we touched our guitars, we'd get these electrical shocks. Blue sparks were flying out of our guitars."

Despite the sparking, the Dead's set never caught fire. After opening with a few minutes of "St. Stephen," the band segued into Merle Haggard's "Mama Tried." But after "High Time," there was a 10-minute delay as the band tried to sort out various technical difficulties. They finally continued with "Dark Star" and closed with a cover of Bobby "Blue" Bland's "Turn On Your Love Light."

Between the delays and the Dead's penchant for playing extended numbers, the set lasted 90 minutes. Although the band members were unhappy with their performance, they could nonetheless joke about it. As they left the stage, Garcia cracked to one of the band's managers, Jon McIntire, "It's nice to know that you can blow the most important gig of your career and it doesn't really matter."

None of the band's set was

Joe Cocker

Woodstock Set List

1. "Dear Landlord"
2. "Something's Coming On"
3. "Do I Still Figure in Your Life"
4. "Feelin' Alright"
5. "Just Like a Woman"
6. "Let's Go Get Stoned"
7. "I Don't Need No Doctor"
8. "I Shall Be Released"
9. "Hitchcock Railway"
10 "Something to Say"
11. "With a Little Help from My Friends"

EVERETT COLLECTION

EVERETT COLLECTION; BACKGROUND: EVERETT COLLECTION

Jimi Hendrix

Woodstock Set List

1. "Introduction"
2. "Message to Love"
3. "Getting My Heart Back Together Again" > "Hear My Train a-Comin'"
4. "Spanish Castle Magic"
5. "Red House"
6. "Mastermind"
7. "Lover Man"
8. "Foxy Lady"
9. "Beginning" > "Jam Back at the House"
10. "Izabella"
11. "Gypsy Woman"
12. "Fire"
13. "Voodoo Child (Slight Return)"
14. "Stepping Stone"
15. "Star Spangled Banner"
16. "Purple Haze"
17. "Woodstock Improvisation"
18. "Villanova Junction"
19. "Hey Joe"

featured in the Woodstock film and soundtrack issued at the time. But 40 years later, two tracks sneaked out. "Turn on Your Love Light" appears among the bonus material on the *Woodstock 40th Anniversary Director's Cut* DVD, while the box set *Woodstock — 40 Years On: Back to Yasgur's Farm* features "Dark Star."

The Altamont Speedway Free Festival, Dec. 6, 1969

The free concert at Altamont Speedway in Tracy, Calif., was supposed to be a counterpart to the Woodstock festival, a "Woodstock West" that would generate the same kind of positive, groovy vibes. Instead, the overall disorganization of the event led not to peace and love, but violence and murder. At the time, *Rolling Stone* magazine called it "rock and roll's all-time worst day … a day when everything went perfectly wrong."

The Dead were involved with the creation of the festival. Co-manager Rock Scully met the Rolling Stones when he visited London in 1967 as he was scouting out places to stage a free concert featuring San Francisco bands. He suggested the Stones consider performing a free concert in California. The band didn't express much interest at the time, but that changed after the Stones began a tour of America in November 1969.

The Stones hadn't toured America for over three years, and there was much anticipation for the shows. There was also criticism over the high ticket prices. Hoping to mollify the criticism, the Stones announced they would cap their tour with a free show in San Francisco. Scully suggested they play an unannounced show at a venue like the Fillmore, but the Stones wanted to play a larger-scale event. Golden Gate Park was considered, but when permits couldn't be obtained, a new site was

Mick Jagger signs autographs before the infamous show at Altamont Motor Speedway.

The Rolling Stones

Altamont Set List

1. "Jumpin' Jack Flash"
2. "Carol" (Chuck Berry cover)
3. "Sympathy for the Devil" (Stopped then restarted)
4. "The Sun Is Shining" (Jimmy Reed cover)
5. "Stray Cat Blues"
6. "Love in Vain" (Robert Johnson cover)
7. "Under My Thumb" (Stopped then restarted)
8. "Brown Sugar" (first performance ever)
9. "Midnight Rambler"
10. "Live with Me"
11. "Gimme Shelter"
12. "Little Queenie" (Chuck Berry cover)
13. "(I Can't Get No) Satisfaction"
14. "Honky Tonk Women"
15. "Street Fighting Man"

found at the Sears Point Raceway in Sonoma, just north of San Francisco.

Then a new problem arose. The event was going to be filmed by the documentary team of Albert and David Maysles — who were making a movie of the Stones' tour, which would be released as *Gimme Shelter* — and the raceway's parent company wanted to be involved in the deal. On being told no, the company revoked permission to use the venue. A new venue had to be found with only two days until the show. Dick Carter, owner of Altamont Speedway, offered his site for the concert, eager for the publicity. Scully and Woodstock producer Michael Lang, who had been brought in to assist, toured the site by helicopter. Scully described the place as looking like a "war zone" to journalist David Curry, but with time running out, the festival was moved to Altamont.

In the rush to pull the show together, there wasn't time to arrange for proper facilities.

AP PHOTO

Another issue was the stage, which was built low to the ground. It had been designed for the Sears Point site, where it would have been on top of a hill, making activity around the stage easier to control. At Altamont, it was located on the bottom of an incline.

In a fateful decision, Scully and Stones' tour manager Sam Cutler met with Pete Knell of the San Francisco chapter of the Hell's Angels motorcycle club about providing some security. The Dead had occasionally used a few Angels at its shows to guard the generators. Knell said the Angels didn't want to provide formal security, but Cutler assured him the Stones would take care of that aspect and that the Angels would just have to protect the stage. In lieu of payment, the Angels were provided with $500 worth of beer.

Despite Cutler's promises, little professional security was present at Altamont. The Angels were the most visible security force, and fights began breaking out from the moment the first act, Santana, took the stage. Heightening the tension was the fact that there was no proper stage barrier.

The Angels placed a member's motorcycle in front of the stage to provide some protection, but when the crowd knocked it over, fights broke out again. And when Jefferson Airplane's Marty Balin jumped into the crowd to try and stop the fighting during the Airplane's set, he was swiftly felled by an Angel's punch, knocking him out cold.

In a last-ditch effort to try and keep things from spiraling totally out of control, Scully told the Dead, who were scheduled to play right before the Stones, that they shouldn't perform. "I encouraged everybody to just give up and get the Stones on stage as quickly as possible," Scully told Curry. "It was getting worse, it was a terrible thing. It was gonna get dark, and we had no lighting, and people were going to be stumbling around in the dark. We really couldn't go on."

So the Dead, at the last minute, didn't play the festival they had helped organize. Altamont is remembered not for its music, but for the death of 18-year-old Meredith Hunter, who was fatally stabbed during an altercation with the Angels during the Stones' set. Two weeks later, during a show at the Fillmore, the Dead unveiled a song about the event, "New Speedway Boogie," which made the sad observation, "Things went down we don't understand, but I think in time we will."

"If the name 'Woodstock' has come to denote the flower of one phase of the youth culture, 'Altamont' has come to mean the end of it," Ralph Gleason later wrote in *Esquire*. As much as Woodstock had raised hopes for the '60s generation, Altamont had cruelly dashed them. The Dead would go on to play numerous festivals over the course of their career; thankfully, none would cast the dark shadow that Altamont did. ●

Members of the Hell's Angels Motorcycle Club beat an audience member during the Altamont Speedway Free Festival.

MARY EVANS/RONALD GRANT/EVERETT COLLECTION; BACKGROUND: EVERETT COLLECTION

Dark Star

BLAME IT ON THE BLACK STAR

One recently advanced scientific theory holds that the first stars in the universe were massive stars fueled by dark matter. The team of astrophysicists that worked on the theory included several Grateful Dead fans, who insisted that these stars be called "dark stars" in tribute to the band. "I prefer 'brown giant' ... but 'dark star' is catchier," said one researcher. When Hunter wrote the lyrics he was most likely thinking of a star's collapse and death, "pouring its light into ashes," after which it becomes a black dwarf or black hole.

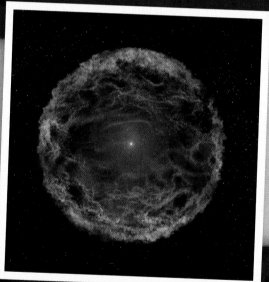

Experimental composer John Oswald was encouraged by the Dead to create a version of "Dark Star" edited together from over 100 performances. The two-hour song was released as the album *Grayfolded*.

....

Some artists who have covered "Dark Star" include guitarist Henry Kaiser, jazz saxophonist David Murray, the David Grisman Quintet and Garth Hudson of the Band.

....

"Dark Star" was the first song Robert Hunter wrote lyrics for. He wrote the lyrics quickly after hearing the Dead experimenting with chords Garcia had written.

Robert Hunter:

"I was very impressed with T.S. Eliot around the time I was writing 'Dark Star.' One line, 'Shall we go, you and I, while we can, through the transitive nightfall of diamonds' is based on a line from 'The Love Song of J. Alfred Prufrock' — 'Let us go then, you and I, when the evening is spread out against the sky.'" Hunter later clarified: "I don't have any idea what 'the transitive nightfall of diamonds' means. It sounded good at the time."

SUPERNOVA: WIKI COMMONS

Live/Dead
1969

SONG WRITTEN BY: the Grateful Dead; lyrics by Robert Hunter

VOCAL: Jerry Garcia

PERFORMED 236 TIMES. In the '60s, "Dark Star" was played at almost every show. By the early '70s, it was often over 30 minutes long, and occasionally over 40 minutes, with other songs sometimes played in the middle. "Dark Star" went on hiatus between 1974 and December '78, and then was performed only very occasionally, becoming renowned for its rarity. After a five-year gap it was played Oct. 9, 1989, and after that was played semiregularly.

FIRST PERFORMED: Jan. 17, 1968, at the Carousel Ballroom in San Francisco

LAST PERFORMED: March 30, 1994, at the Omni in Atlanta, Ga.

KEY LYRIC: "Shall we go, you and I, while we can?"

In one famous concert at the Nassau Coliseum in New York on March 29, 1990, saxophonist Branford Marsalis joined the Dead for a set. Marsalis recalled, "They said, 'Hey, let's play 'Dark Star.'' I was like, 'Oh, I don't know the song.' They said, 'Oh, you'll love it. It's right up your alley.' They started playing the song and the audience went bananas. … I'm going, 'Okay, this must be an anthem.'"

Tom Constanten:

"'Dark Star' is going on all the time. It's going on right now. You don't begin it so much as enter it. You don't end it so much as leave it."

Jerry Garcia:

"'Dark Star' is so little, you know? It's only like three or four lines. Really, 'Dark Star' is a little of everything we do. … What happened to 'Dark Star' was, it went into everything; everything's got a little 'Dark Star' in it. … It's a minimal tune; there's really no tune — just a couple of lines and that's it. So it's hard for me to relate to what it is about 'Dark Star' that people like, apart from the part that we get weird in it. … It's an envelope for me, not really a song."

Italian director Michelangelo Antonioni used part of "Dark Star" in the soundtrack for his 1970 film *Zabriskie Point*, an English-language box-office dud that has become a cult film.

"Dark Star" was released as a single in 1968, in a studio version that was less than three minutes long. It didn't reach the charts. When it first appeared on a record, *Live/Dead*, it was jammed for over 20 minutes.

TOP: KERRY MALONEY/AP PHOTO; BOTTOM: AP PHOTO

TOP: PHOTOSHOT/EVERETT COLLECTION. MIDDLE: BILL FOLEY/AP PHOTO. BOTTOM: SUSANA MILLMAN. BACKGROUND: MAOOOLTEE/SHUTTERSTOCK

The Dead's Adventures Abroad

The quintessentially American band had mixed success in the Old World.

BY PETER SMITH AND IAN INGLIS

Of all the bands to have emerged from the tangled roots of rock 'n' roll, the Grateful Dead are perhaps the most openly and defiantly American — in their cultural references, style of music and general outlook. Jerry Garcia's reflection on the alliance between the band and its fans invoked a shared sense of American mythology: "It's an adventure you can still have in America … you can't hop a freight, but you can chase the Grateful Dead around."

SUSANA MILLMAN

The Dead's repertoire included 144 songs, 90 of which they performed during their 1990 tour of Europe.

Trains to Tulsa, floods in Texas, scores to settle and silver dollars: Lyrically, the Dead drew heavily on that same American mythology. Pigpen declared, "The songs we play are our history — the American West."

Phil Lesh readily admitted, "We weren't sure how what we did would travel. It is a uniquely American experience."

But the Dead did travel to Europe, playing 60 shows, often at smaller venues, over seven different trips. It's a tiny number compared to the more than 2,000 times American fans had a chance to see the Dead live and in person, but for the band's European fans, long regarded as among the most passionate, knowledgeable and articulate supporters of the Dead, those shows have special significance.

Quizzed about the differences between American Deadheads and their European counterparts, Garcia said, "It's possible European fans are a little more studied — that is, they know more about things generally, about music in general,

what our roots are, and so forth … they seem a little more interested in that side of things."

1970-71
"We Played and the People Came"

The first San Francisco rock musicians to visit Europe were Jefferson Airplane, accompanied by the Doors, in September 1968. Subsequent plans for a free concert in London's Hyde Park in 1968 featuring the Dead and Airplane came to nothing. It was not until May 1970 that the Dead made their European debut, not on tour, but in a single two-hour performance in front of around 45,000 fans at the Hollywood Music Festival in Staffordshire, England.

One year later, the Dead traveled to France for another one-off appearance, in Auvers-sur-Oise near Paris, for an audience of barely 200 people. Garcia explained, "We went over there to do a big festival, a free festival they were gonna have, but the festival was rained

JORGEN ANGEL/IDOLS PHOTOSHOT/EVERETT COLLECTION

what's regarded by many as a peak year in the band's career, the 1972 tour itself is seen as a musical superlative. It was the first full tour in which Donna Jean Godchaux was established as a full member rather than a guest vocalist. Sadly, it was to be Pigpen's last tour. Traveling against medical advice, his contribution was nevertheless important and memorable, and included regular performances of "Mr. Charlie," "Chinatown Shuffle," "Good Lovin'," and "Turn on Your Lovelight." A few weeks after the band returned to the U.S., he made his final appearance, playing but not singing, and died less than a year later of cirrhosis.

While Pigpen's earthy raps involved tales of drinking, debauchery and breaking the law, the other band members, especially Garcia and Lesh, were keen to explore the sonic depths of psychedelia via performances of "Dark Star" and "The Other One." At the Bickershaw Festival in England, the band played a 63-minute jam that uniquely included both songs. At Rotterdam, the Dead gave their longest-ever performance of "Dark Star," clocking in at 47 minutes.

In addition, the lachrymose "Looks Like Rain," released on Weir's *Ace* album during the tour, provided Garcia with a rare opportunity to play pedal steel guitar, something he would not do again with the band until the Dead's 1987 tour with Bob Dylan.

The 1972 tour took place in a variety of venues. In Copenhagen, Amsterdam, Dusseldorf and Frankfurt, the performances were in

Jerry Garcia and Bob Weir play with the rest of the Grateful Dead in Copenhagen, Denmark, in 1972.

out. It flooded. We stayed at this little chateau that Chopin once lived in … so, we decided to play at the chateau itself, out in the back, in the grass, with a swimming pool, just play into the hills. We didn't even play to hippies, we played to a handful of townspeople in Auvers. We played and the people came — the chief of police, the fire department, just everybody. It was an event and everybody just had a hell of a time — got drunk, fell in the pool. It was great."

1972
Bolos and Bozos

The Grateful Dead's first full European tour took place in April and May 1972, when the Dead gave 22 performances across six countries. Taking place in

concert halls whose histories were steeped in classical music. Lesh later recalled, "I remember that tour clearly. In Hamburg, we played in the hall where Brahms played. In Paris, I literally felt the spirits of Chopin and Debussy. I think that made us play better. I remember being on."

In Bremen, the band prerecorded a relatively short set in the Beat Club TV studio. In Luxembourg, an audience of around 500 attended a show in Radio Luxembourg's auditorium that was broadcast live across Europe. In France, the outdoor concert in Lille became a free event after the band had been forced to cancel its scheduled indoor show because an equipment truck had been sabotaged in Paris. A more conventional outdoor event was the Bickershaw Festival, where the Dead played for two minutes short of four hours — the longest performance on a tour where shows would typically run for over three hours.

The band, accompanied by friends and family, treated the seven-week tour as an extended vacation. As well as sightseeing in all the major

cities, they visited Stonehenge in England and medieval castles in Sweden and Germany. The entourage traveled in two coaches, the Bozo Bus, for the party animals, and the Bolo Bus, for the more sedate members of the party. Lesh recalled, "I was on the Bolo Bus. You got more sleep on that one. Most of the roadies were Bozos. Jerry and Bob were on that bus. Pigpen was on the Bolo Bus with me." The band's crew brought a large supply of rubber masks, which they wore on the road in the spirit of the Merry Pranksters — and which the entire band wore during the televised segment of their Copenhagen show.

1974

Tired and Fractious

In September 1974, the Dead paid a brief visit to Europe, during which they performed three shows in England, one in Germany and three in France. Three more planned shows, in

The 1990 tour was to be the Dead's last in Europe.

SUSANA MILLMAN

Amsterdam and France, were cancelled. The rising costs and troublesome logistics of hauling their Wall of Sound PA system around Europe cemented the band's decision, confirmed the following month, to cease touring for a while.

Keyboardist Ned Lagin joined the band for this tour, and a Phil-and-Ned session of avant-garde electronic music (not always readily appreciated by audiences) bridged the gap between the Dead's sets.

By the time of the 1974 tour, the Dead's repertoire had changed significantly from their previous visit. Material was introduced from two recent studio albums, *Wake of the Flood* and *From the Mars Hotel*. The lengthy second set jams continued, but now sprang from material such as "Eyes of the World."

On this occasion, wives, partners and family were left at home, and accounts of excessive drug consumption quickly circulated. Manager Rock Scully recalled how the fallout from the band's and crew's use of cocaine and other drugs resulted in constant bickering and fighting. By the time of the first show, things were already so out of hand that roadies Rex Jackson and Ramrod challenged everyone — band and crew — to throw their drug stashes on the floor. The stashes were reluctantly presented and duly incinerated.

1978

Victims of Punk?

In September 1978, the Dead famously played for three nights at the base of the Great Pyramid in Giza, Egypt. The attitude of the Egyptian authorities, who gave permission for the unusual event, was in stark contrast to that of the British authorities who in 1972 rejected the band's request to play at Stonehenge. To recoup some of the costs incurred in flying 174 members of the extended Dead family from California to Egypt, a series of 11 shows was planned in Europe.

When these shows were cancelled, no formal explanation was given. It's likely that potential ticket sales were disappointingly low. The musical soundtrack of Europe had been substantially rewritten by the punk revolution. To punk audiences and performers alike — especially in the U.K. — any bands with roots in the 1960s were dismissed as out-of-touch and irrelevant. Johnny Rotten's assertion that the Sex Pistols confused and bewildered a stagnant musical scene singled out the Dead for particular criticism: "It was much like putting the Bay City Rollers on the same stage as the Grateful Dead, and expecting them to both play similarly. Or at least expecting both to be as musically competent — if you view the Grateful Dead as competent in any shape or form."

The animosity, at least in certain quarters, lingered for several years. During the Dead's next visit, in 1981, *New Musical Express*'s Paul Morley provocatively accused Garcia of being "part of a perpetuation of bland, blanketing myths," and asked, "Does it upset you that I don't dig you?" Garcia's reply was disarmingly frank: "No. I don't give a damn." It was estimated that the article lost the publication between 10,000 and 30,000 readers.

The Sex Pistols and the rise of punk rock helped curb the Dead's appeal and presence in European venues.

AP PHOTO

With an improvement in Jerry Garcia's health in 1990, the Dead were able to achieve more fluid, inventive performances.

1981

Rainbow and Rockpalast

The Dead visited Europe twice in 1981, by which time the momentum of punk had considerably dissipated. Their first visit, in March, consisted of a four-night run at London's Rainbow Theatre and one night in Essen, Germany.

The Rainbow had an illustrious rock history — it was where Jimi Hendrix first set fire to his guitar (in June 1967). A former movie theater, its ground-floor seating had been removed, leaving room for audiences to stand, sit or dance. For many fans, this relatively small venue was an ideal environment for a Dead concert.

The Essen gig was broadcast live on radio and on WDR-TV's *Rockpalast* show, seen across much of Europe. Pete Townshend of The Who joined the Dead for the concluding five songs.

The Dead's 1981 tour introduced keyboardist Brent Mydland to European audiences and reintroduced percussionist Mickey Hart, who had left the band from 1971 to 1974. Kreutzmann and Hart had developed a regular drum session midway through the second set that allowed the other members of the band to take a short break. At the final Rainbow show and at Essen, the drummers were joined by the Flying Karamazov Brothers, who performed their juggling and comedy act while playing various percussion instruments.

The band returned to Europe in September and October to give 14 shows in six countries. Their opening four-night run at London's Rainbow was followed by shows in Denmark, the Netherlands, Germany, France and their only show ever in Spain. The songs and structure of the shows were similar to those in March.

The most celebrated shows were at Amsterdam's Melk Weg (Milky Way) Club, renowned at the time for a menu that included hashish. Finding themselves there on a free day, Garcia and Weir spontaneously performed a seven-song acoustic duet in the intimate 400-seat club. A few days later, following the cancellation of two shows in France, the whole band performed two impromptu gigs at the club. Playing on borrowed instruments and equipment and freed from the constraints of scheduled shows, the band resurrected songs which took them back to their early days — "Spoonful," "Hully Gully," "Gloria" — and Weir launched into the first post-Pigpen version of "Turn on Your Lovelight."

The final show, in Barcelona, prompted the band to perform "Spanish Jam" (loosely based on Miles Davis' "Sketches of Spain"). By this time, touring and unchecked drug use were having a serious effect on Garcia's performances, and the rest of the band presented him with a written ultimatum — drafted by Lesh and signed by all — urging him to clean up his act.

1990

Changing Times

The recruitment of keyboardist Vince Welnick to replace Brent Mydland, the temporary addition of acclaimed pianist Bruce Hornsby

SUSANA MILLMAN

Deadheads in Europe

European audiences were generally resigned to the absence of major American acts. Elvis Presley never performed outside North America, and from 1966 to 1974 Bob Dylan made just one European appearance.

Unlike the Beach Boys, the Byrds, CSNY and the Eagles, the Dead never pursued overseas hit singles, and only three of their albums entered the U.K. top 40 album chart, with *American Beauty* peaking at No. 27 in 1971.

The Dead's dearth of European appearances didn't change after Garcia's death. There have been only three European visits — two tours by Bob Weir's band RatDog (19 shows in 2002 and 2003) and two concerts by Phil Lesh & the Family Band in London in 2014.

And yet, European fans of the Grateful Dead have remained intensely loyal. During the 1970s and '80s, European fans followed the Dead's activities through fanzines such as *Spiral Light* and *Dark Star*, and bonds were formed through acquiring and trading tapes of the band's shows.

While digital archives have replaced fanzines and tapes, European fans continue to celebrate the Dead in a very physical and communal sense. Tribute bands are popular. Among the best known are Cosmic Charlies (U.K.); Deadicace (France); Cosmic Finger and Dead Again (Germany); and AoxoToxoA (Switzerland).

West Coast/psychedelia-themed festivals provide opportunities for the kind of communal gatherings enjoyed by American Deadheads, with European fans decked out in tie-dye and embracing other statements of Deadhead identify and self-expression. The notion of a lifestyle built around the Grateful Dead has continued to flourish across Europe.

and Garcia's improved physical condition led to a more fluid and inventive level of playing on the Dead's final visit to Europe in October and November 1990. The band played 11 shows in four European countries — Germany, France, the U.K. and, for the first time, Sweden.

After touring the U.S. heavily for the preceding two years, the band approached this visit as something of a holiday. The more relaxed atmosphere prompted Lesh, Garcia and Hart to bring along some of their children to see the sights. Lesh happily watched his 4-year-old son Grahame hammer out a piece of masonry from the Berlin Wall just two weeks after the reunification of Germany.

The material for this tour was augmented by selections from the band's *In the Dark* and *Built to Last* albums. By 1990, the band's repertoire had expanded to 144 songs, and during the tour the band performed more than 90 of them, with only a few featured more than once. The Dead's versions of two Hornsby songs ("Valley Road" and "Stander") also debuted during the tour.

During the years since the 1981 European visit, the shows' second set "Drums/Space" sequence had become increasingly complex. The segment typically lasted some 20 minutes, beginning with conventional percussion before the drummers moved to the device known as the Beam to produce a vast range of improvised and exotic sounds. The sequence then moved into "Space" as the non-drumming members of the band returned to the stage one by one.

This was the most adventurous section of each show, reflecting the band's willingness to enter uncharted and experimental musical territory each night — although for some fans, both European and American, it was an unwarranted slice of self-indulgence. The content of "Drums/Space" was always unpredictable, but a particularly strange episode occurred at the first London show when a private mobile phone conversation between two women was somehow picked up and broadcast.

Playing in London on the night of Halloween, the Dead's encore was, appropriately, their version of Warren Zevon's "Werewolves of London." On the final night the band was unable to resist playing Dylan's "Maggie's Farm" — ("I ain't gonna work on Maggie's farm no more") a pointed shot at U.K. Prime Minister Margaret Thatcher's conservative policies. ●

Aoxomoxoa
1969

SONG WRITTEN BY: Jerry Garcia and Phil Lesh; lyrics by Robert Hunter

VOCALS: Jerry Garcia, Bob Weir and Phil Lesh

PERFORMED 168 TIMES. Most commonly played in the "Dark Star" → "St. Stephen" → "The Eleven" suite. Later on it was often paired in a medley with "Not Fade Away." Played frequently up until October 1971, it then went on hiatus for five years, returning in a slower version in June '76. The Dead stopped playing it again in January '78, except for a brief revival at the end of '78 and three final performances in October '83.

FIRST PERFORMED: June 14, 1968, at the Fillmore East in New York City

LAST PERFORMED: Oct. 31, 1983, at the Marin Veterans' Memorial Auditorium in San Rafael, Calif.

KEY LYRIC: "One man gathers what another man spills."

The "calliope woman" in the lyrics could be a reference to Calliope, the muse of eloquence and epic poetry in Greek myth. She is often depicted holding a lyre or other instrument in ancient art. Then again, it could be a woman playing a calliope — a loud, piano-like instrument as sociated with circuses. Or, Hunter may have just liked the sound of the word.

....

The Dead recorded a trippy 8-track version of "St. Stephen" that can be heard at archive.org. The album version was recorded on a 16-track machine.

CALLIOPE: CHARLES MEYNIER/WIKI COMMONS

St. Stephen

Jefferson Airplane used the main riff from "St. Stephen" in their songs "Volunteers" and "We Can Be Together."

"WELL HE MAY AND HE MAY DECLINE"

Among Dead fans, the song became notorious as a popular favorite that the band never played. Bob Weir admitted at one '72 show, "We done forgot 'St. Stephen' … we can't play it anymore. We don't know how." He teased one audience in '73: "We had to quit doing it 'cause you liked it too much."

Now and then the Dead brought it back, but Garcia explained in the '80s that the band was tired of the song: "People ask us, why don't you do 'St. Stephen' anymore? The truth is, we did it to death when we did do it. … People who missed it, that's too bad, you know? We may never do it again. It's one of those things that doesn't perform that well — we were able to make it work then because we had the power of conviction."

Robert Hunter:

"I had been working on this a long time before I gave it to the Grateful Dead. … It's still one of my favorites. I didn't know who the real St. Stephen was until I wrote it."

Garcia called it a "goofy" song: "It's got little idiosyncrasies and verses that are different from each other. … It's a piece of material that is unnecessarily difficult. It's been made tricky. It's got a bridge in the middle that doesn't really fit in. … The verses aren't interchangeable, you have to do them in order. … A song like 'St. Stephen' is a cop; it's our musical policeman. If we don't do it the way it wants to go, it doesn't work at all."

St. Stephen was the first Christian martyr, an early deacon stoned to death in Jerusalem for blasphemy. His story is told in chapters 6 and 7 in the Book of Acts of the New Testament. Garcia's funeral service was held in St. Stephen's Episcopal Church in Belvedere, Calif.

Legend has it that the song is about Stephen Gaskin, a popular San Francisco guru during the late '60s and a speaker on spirituality and drugs. Gaskin is best known for creating The Farm, an alternative community in Tennessee.

ABOVE: AP PHOTO. RIGHT: NAMBASSA TRUST AND PETER TERRY, HTTP://WWW.NAMBASSA.COM/WIKI COMMONS

THE AGE OF REAG

The Grateful Dead thrived with a rival Californian in the Oval Office.

BY PETER RICHARDSON

It's difficult to imagine someone less like the Grateful Dead than Ronald Reagan. But as California governor and U.S. president, Reagan was an ideal foil for the Dead and their project.

As Reagan campaigned for governor in the summer of 1966, the Grateful Dead were making music, partying, skinny-dipping and ignoring politics at their bucolic retreat in Marin County. But if the revelers weren't interested in politics, the opposite wasn't true; in fact, youth culture played a significant role in California's elections that year. "Their signs say, 'Make love, not war,'" Reagan said about campus activists, "but it didn't look like they could do either." Hippies were another favorite target. "We have some hippies in California," he told out-of-state audiences. "For those of you who don't know what a hippie is, he's a fellow who dresses like Tarzan, has hair like Jane and smells like Cheetah."

Despite the conservative backlash that powered Reagan's 1966 victory that November, the Grateful Dead thrived during his two terms as governor. They released their first commercially

BACKGROUND: STRELOV/SHUTTERSTOCK; REAGAN: LARRY STODDARD/AP PHOTO

and critically successful albums, and except for a brief hiatus in the mid-1970s, they toured relentlessly and became one of the nation's most popular live bands. Reagan left Sacramento in 1974 and began his march to the White House. After an unsuccessful bid for the GOP nomination in 1976, he prevailed over incumbent Jimmy Carter in 1980.

It's All Right

While Deadheads are associated with liberal causes, Dead fans are hardly all cut from the same cloth. Future conservative commentators Ann Coulter and Tucker Carlson were among those who welcomed Reagan's ascent. Some conservative sentiment was even present in the band's inner circle. Lyricist John Perry Barlow, for example, helped coordinate Dick Cheney's 1978 Congressional campaign in Wyoming.

But Jerry Garcia, the Dead's lead guitarist, was no Reagan fan. "Oh! Give me a break!" he exclaimed later. "I was shocked when Reagan was elected governor of California! And then, as President, we were embarrassed by the guy. I mean, he wasn't even a good actor."

The Grateful Dead didn't orchestrate a response to Reagan, but his militarization of the drug war in 1982 was deeply unpopular in Dead circles, and the band's key fanzine uncharacteristically exhorted Deadheads to register and vote against Reagan in 1984.

Above: At sunrise on Oct. 6, 1967, hippies in San Francisco began a three-day "wake" for the death of the hippie movement.

Right: Conservative commentators Tucker Carlson and Ann Coulter both count themselves Deadheads.

TOP: AP PHOTO. CARLSON: DAVE ALLOCCA/STARPIX/AP PHOTO. COULTER: LEV RADIN/SHUTTERSTOCK

CHARLES TASNADI/AP PHOTO

Ronald and Nancy Reagan go over an address they were to give jointly on Sept. 13, 1986. The topic in question? The "War on Drugs."

By the time that piece appeared, President Reagan's reelection campaign was in high gear. One television advertisement declared that it was "morning again in America." But the opening verse of "Touch of Grey," which the Dead first performed in 1982, found little to celebrate in that daybreak:

Dawn is breaking everywhere
Light a candle, curse the glare
Draw the curtain, I don't care 'cause
It's all right

The song's political subtext is signaled in the second line, which Garcia contributed. It echoes Adlai Stevenson's 1962 comment that Eleanor Roosevelt would rather "light a candle than curse the darkness."

Although the music for "Touch of Grey" was upbeat, the lyrics lacked the Utopian exuberance of the 1960s. Instead, the world-weary speaker embraces the more modest goal of trying "to keep a little grace." In the age of Reagan, even that goal seemed ambitious, as later verses make clear.

I know the rent is in arrears
The dog has not been fed in years
It's even worse than it appears
But it's all right

The cow is giving kerosene
Kid can't read at seventeen
The words he knows are all obscene
But it's all right

In the face of economic hardship, environmental catastrophe and educational failure, the speaker's repeated assurances ("But it's all

TOP: AP PHOTO. BOTTOM: GUY PALMIOTTO/AP PHOTO

Never considered to be overtly political — and sometimes criticized for it — the Grateful Dead responded to the age of Reagan with some of their most subversive, politically-charged musical statements.

right") only highlight the challenges. Yet the speaker promises to endure: "I will get by / I will survive." A simple pronoun change in the final chorus ("We will get by / We will survive") transformed the song into an anthem.

When the band opened a 1986 concert in Oakland with "Touch of Grey," the audience went wild. There were at least two reasons for their glee. Garcia had survived a serious health scare earlier that year, and Deadheads could reasonably believe that their most cherished ideal — community — would survive Reagan. More than two decades after the Dead's formation, "Touch of Grey" became their first top-10 single.

After Garcia's Death

When asked about Reagan, Garcia claimed that history was on the Dead's side. But the tension between their project and Reagan's was even clearer in the immediate aftermath of Garcia's death in 1995. "The band has prospered

COREY STRULLER/AP PHOTO

Though many on the political right criticized the band for their influence on popular culture, the Dead were a quintessentially American band with American ideals.

as the emblem of an era and is complicit in the continuing consequences of the era," George Will wrote in *Newsweek*. "Around it has hung an aroma of disdain for inhibitions on recreational uses of drugs and sex. During the band's nearly 30-year life, the costs of 'liberation' from such inhibitions have been made manifest in millions of shattered lives and miles of devastated cities."

William F. Buckley also seized on Garcia's death to scold the counterculture. He wrote that after a *National Review* intern attended and enjoyed a Grateful Dead show, his work fell off, and he moved to South America to teach English. "Jerry Garcia didn't help this young man," Buckley wrote. "We did not hear again from him, except after an interval of five years or so, when we learned he had married again, this time a native, and gone off to live in the hills. Question before the house: Is Jerry Garcia in some way responsible for this?" According to Buckley, the answer was yes. He asserted that Garcia had "killed, if that's the right word for such as our intern, a lot of people."

It was an extraordinary claim, but it wasn't

clear that it would prevail even at *National Review*. Deroy Murdock, who wrote for the magazine's online edition, saw it otherwise. "Jerry Garcia's abuse of his bear-like body should teach all of us a lesson on the value of moderation," he wrote. "But the rest of his life — from the music to which he remained true for over 30 years to the spirit of freedom that still permeates the community he led — amiably embodied an all-American ideal: the pursuit of happiness."

Murdock's conclusion was also consistent with Garcia's views. "We're basically Americans, and we like America," he said. "We like the things about being able to express outrageous amounts of freedom."

Although the Dead offered a fully formed alternative to Reagan's vision, a large part of their appeal arose not from their resistance to American culture, but rather from their uncanny ability to tap its inexhaustible Utopian energies. Despite the flak they took from some Reagan supporters, the Dead were as American as apple pie. ●

ABOVE: TOM COSTELLO/AP PHOTO; GUITAR: BALU/SHUTTERSTOCK

Missed chances marked the collaboration between the Grateful Dead and Bob Dylan.

BY TIM RILEY

Bob Dylan's winding career path crossed with the Grateful Dead's for six shows during the summer of 1987, bringing together two legendary acts that had shared musical sources and audiences for over two decades. The pairing thrilled fans from both camps until the arrival of the stale live album *Dylan & the Dead* in 1989, which dishonored both careers. Debate continues about who's to blame. In Dylan's *Chronicles* memoir, he recounts how the Dead's larger ambitions took him by surprise: "The whole thing might have been a mistake. … I'd have to go someplace for the mentally ill and think about it."

But it might have gone differently. On many levels, the pairing had mystical appeal: Dylan and the Dead shared the same windblown tradition, starting with *The Anthology of American Folk Music*, compiled by one of folk's original mad clowns, Harry Smith, and released in 1952 by Folkways Records. This three-LP vinyl set found eager ears in the middle of the century among young Bohemians who intuited a more scattershot history — more freedom, more craziness — than their high school textbooks revealed.

Curiously, Dylan and Garcia heard Smith's compilation as a portal to different creative territories. On the East Coast, where Dylan hitched from Minnesota to shake the hand of his bed-ridden hero Woody Guthrie, Smith's frame spelled "folk," whereas to the young

TOMBSTONE BLUES

Garcia could hear the rock 'n' roll woven through Dylan's words long before Dylan plugged in his guitar. And Garcia had a flukish insight: Dylan songs got weirder when you danced to them. It makes you wonder how differently Dylan's career might have gone had he come from San Francisco.

Zombie Dylan

Jump cut to the mid-1980s. By the time Dylan dueted with the Dead, he'd do anything to get the needle back in the groove. Even his better aims roused misfires. His 1986 single "Band of the Hand" had a searing bravado that charged a promising tour with Tom Petty's Heartbreakers. But then, in the stretch preceding his induction into the Rock and Roll Hall of Fame in 1988, Dylan starred in the unwatchable *Hearts of Fire* (1987) and left pearls like "Blind

Dylan is an icon of rock 'n' roll, and his musical influence on the Dead can't be denied.

Garcia (ironically named for Broadway tune-smith Jerome Kern), the same deep roots tilted more toward bluegrass and rock 'n' roll.

As the American rock scene sputtered in uncertain shocks and starts after the Beatles hit, West Coasters waited impatiently for Dylan to go electric. When he finally offended traditionalists by singing "Like a Rolling Stone" during his historic electric set at the Newport Folk Festival in 1965, Garcia's Uptown Jug Companions had already morphed into the Warlocks, and Dylan's acoustic "It's All Over Now, Baby Blue" was soon an electrified Warlocks staple.

Willie McTell" and "Foot of Pride" off duds like *Knocked Out Loaded* and *Down in the Groove* (1986 and 1988), albums that combined overwritten songs with drab production.

Looking back over his 50-year career, several factors define Dylan's recurring zombie slumps. The first is his lack of vocal commitment. While his obdurate phrasing defines his delivery, it just as easily veers into indifference, and after his gospel phase (1979-1981), Dylan steered songs straight into their own ditches. Listeners who bemoaned his born-again odes now longed for any kind of emotional investment. His dispassion

AP PHOTO

The Biblical Period

Jerry Garcia played with Bob Dylan at a June 1981 Warfield Theatre show in San Francisco, during a period when many rock luminaries kept their distance from Dylan because he was performing Christian music. This appearance made a big impression on Dylan. It's noteworthy that several of the songs Dylan and the Dead played together were from his gospel period, including "Slow Train," "Man of Peace" and "Gotta Serve Somebody" (with lyrics like "It may be the devil or it may be the Lord, but you're gonna have to serve somebody").

deflated his better lyrics, and lesser stanzas dissolved completely. Half the pleasure of listening to early Dylan lay in the vocal suspense: He willfully stretched out phrases and kept you guessing where words would land. Even after listening to his recordings thousands of times, each new hearing yielded fresh meanings.

The second factor in Dylan's post-gospel phase of meandering indifference was that his sense of humor got waylaid by a yawning fog of philosophical arrogance.

Finally, when it comes to producing a record, Dylan can be the worst judge of his own material. His aura intimidates those around him, and few challenge even his more self-destructive choices. When it came time to assemble the live album capturing the best of Dylan and the Dead's set, Dylan's flaws held sway.

An Album to Forget

Part of what's vexing about *Dylan & the Dead* is how good it might have been if things had gone differently both on and off the stage. Dylan, a giant peculiarity of a singer who relies on vocal mood swings and serendipity, seemed perfectly poised to pilot a band that really never had a great lead vocalist. Turn this turkey album upside down: It's a wonder the Dead versions ever got to sounding this polished, this assured, given that they were still guessing at keys and tempos and Dylan needed prompting on his own lyrics. Imagine what might have been with adequate rehearsal time and motivation.

The members of the Dead were thrilled to finally share the stage with Dylan, and they mapped out sparkling arrangements at the band's Club Front in San Rafael in May 1987.

The colaborative album *Dylan & the Dead* didn't live up to the promise the pairing showed on stage.

SUSANA MILLMAN

As the recordings of the rehearsals show (available at archive.org), when Dylan and the Dead played together without any audience, there was magic in the room.

Only on *Dylan & the Dead*'s "Knockin' On Heaven's Door," where Dylan sings behind the bar to trade fours against the Dead's gospel chorus, does the promise of this pairing show through. It's the only time on the album where Dylan holds out his notes, and he pulls lines toward something unexpected, eerie, frightening even, as if he's glimpsing his own late-period themes: death, decay and what to put on his own tombstone. Garcia's guitar commentary here defies description: He emerges from the fog, more disturbing even than the fathomless icon he stands next to.

Dylan is at his worst on tracks like "Slow Train" and "Gotta Serve Somebody," where Old Testament severity sinks the beat like a stone. Worse yet, Dylan can't pull out of this stodgy mode even for a delight like "I Want You," where guilty undertakers lead the parade with the Queen of Spades' chambermaid. It seems a tart choice for the Dylan-Dead pairing, but it never connects. As usual, one motivation to go back to this music comes from Garcia's guitar, which slings curious and sprightly lines, but also wanders so that Garcia seems at times to be playing in time with some better version of the song that he hears only in his head.

The rotting core of the record, "Joey," opens side two. Lester Bangs famously called the number "one of the most mindlessly amoral pieces of romanticist [BS] ever recorded." For kicks, try playing find-the-beat along with both drummers, and then ponder whether Dylan's playing dodgeball with his players.

Grateful Dead scholars argue persuasively that the band had to go along with Dylan's choices for *Dylan & The Dead*'s tracks, cutting what many at these shows report as inspired moments. Garcia also disagreed with Dylan's ideas for how to mix the tracks. Video and audio recordings of Dylan and the Dead playing

DEREK STORM/EVERETT COLLECTION

The Never-Ending Tour

For Dylan, the six shows he did with the Dead in 1987 had a profound impact. Hearing the Dead's imaginative approach to his older material was reinvigorating for Dylan, who was inspired to find new arrangements for some of the classics in his songbook. More importantly, the Dead's commitment to touring inspired Dylan, who has toured almost constantly since those shows with the Dead. As Dylan said, "You're either a player, or you're not a player. It didn't occur to me until we did those shows with the Grateful Dead. If you just go out every three years or so like I was doing for a while, that's when you lose touch. If you're going to be a performer, you've got to give it your all."

> "He's funny … he doesn't have a conception about two things that are very important in music: starting and ending a song. Really. The middle of the song is great; the beginning and ending are nowhere."
>
> — Jerry Garcia on Bob Dylan

The Dead Play Dylan

The Grateful Dead often played Dylan tunes, but no one song became a concert staple. The Dead pulled most heavily from Dylan's mid-'60s masterpieces, *Highway 61 Revisited* and *Blonde on Blonde*, as well as his *Basement Tapes* period in 1967 when he was collaborating with the Band. The following list shows which Dylan songs the Dead covered, as well as how often the Dead played each tune.

146	"When I Paint My Masterpiece"
143	"It's All Over Now, Baby Blue"
124	"Queen Jane Approximately"
118	"All Along the Watchtower"
72	"Knockin' on Heaven's Door"
70	"Stuck Inside of Mobile (with the Memphis Blues Again)"
59	"Quinn the Eskimo (The Mighty Quinn)"
58	"Just Like Tom Thumb's Blues"
58	"Desolation Row"
40	"Maggie's Farm"
10	"She Belongs to Me"
8	"Visions of Johanna"
7	"It Takes a Lot to Laugh, It Takes a Train to Cry"
2	"Ballad of a Thin Man"
1	"Rainy Day Women #12 & 35"; "Don't Think Twice, It's All Right"; "Forever Young"

PRESS ASSOCIATION/AP PHOTO

Dylan and the Band

Dylan's most important partnership with players came with the Band, which he hired to back him on his fabled 1966 tour through England. When he returned to Woodstock, he promptly wiped out on his motorcycle and holed up with these same players for epic sessions that found release almost a decade later as *The Basement Tapes*.

There's no underestimating the effect of the Band's debut album, *Music From Big Pink* (1968), which launched with "Tears of Rage" and closed with "This Wheel's on Fire" and "I Shall Be Released," three defining Dylan covers. Rustic, casual, reserved and understated, the music glided on introspective arrangements, claiming large spaces with minimal gestures and knowing musical glances.

together are easy to find online, and listeners can decide for themselves whether the tour was the disaster that the live album makes it seem.

Covers and Postcards

Luckily, the story doesn't end with *Dylan & the Dead*.

Dead sets often included a "Dylan slot," with the band choosing from one of the many Dylan covers in its catalogue. The Dead mined the Dylan songbook to create many concert staples: "It Takes a Lot to Laugh, It Takes a Train to Cry," "Maggie's Farm," "Stuck Inside of Mobile (with the Memphis Blues Again)," and "Knockin' on Heaven's Door." To the Dead's credit, Dylan tunes always turned into Grateful Dead music when the band played them.

With all the Dead archives online, the boundless *Dick's Picks* series and the Dead's towering Dylan tribute record, *Postcards from the Hanging*, the band left plenty of testaments as to why Dylan's material held such important secrets for them.

On *Postcards*, the definitive Dead-Dylan effort, the band brings new intrigue to one of their own longtime staples, "When I Paint My

Bob Dylan and Tom Petty perform at the Southern Star Amphitheater in Houston on June 20, 1986.

HOUSTON CHRONICLE, BEN DESOTO/AP PHOTO

Masterpiece," a jaunty meditation on fame where Bob Weir plays ringmaster. "Love Minus Zero (No Limit)" features some inimitable Garcia guitar, and Garcia and Weir trade leads on "Maggie's Farm," smiles chasing after one another.

"Stuck Inside of Mobile (with the Memphis Blues Again)" warns about the dangers of mixing amphetamines ("Texas medicine") with alcohol ("railroad gin"): "And like a fool I mixed them / And it strangled up my mind / And now people just get uglier / And I have no sense of time."

Weir peels off lines more like a reporter reading off a ticker tape, too stunned by what's coming out of his mouth to adopt a viewpoint. By the end, he goes delirious as the song summons some prohibited apostasy, inner demons cackling their way out of giddy darkness.

Garcia sings "It Takes a Lot to Laugh, It Takes a Train to Cry," and like his solo version of "Positively 4th Street," he sounds calm, atoning rather than raving, which brings out the song's wispy melody; perhaps it's his looming frame, but his intimate, scratchy voice sidesteps anger. Garcia brings more impassioned nuance to Dylan than Weir, even if his delivery has less strength. And "The Mighty Quinn" might just be the Dead's living koan, a descent into a comic wormhole: "A cat's meow and a cow's moo, I can recite 'em all / Just tell me where it hurts yuh, honey / And I'll tell you who to call." ●

SUSANA MILLMAN

A Lot of Universes

Bob Dylan's respect for the Grateful Dead and its mission came through in his deeply felt eulogy for Garcia in 1995. Deadheads regard it as the very highest honor any peer paid him:

"There's a lot of spaces and advances between The Carter Family, Buddy Holly and, say, Ornette Coleman, a lot of universes, but [Jerry] filled them all without being a member of any school. His playing was moody, awesome, sophisticated, hypnotic and subtle. There's no way to convey the loss. It just digs down really deep."

EFUL DEAD: WIKI COMMONS

American Beauty
1970

SONG WRITTEN BY: Jerry Garcia, Bob Weir and Phil Lesh; lyrics by Robert Hunter

VOCAL: Bob Weir

PERFORMED 530 TIMES. It started out as an acoustic song, but went electric on Oct. 4, 1970. It soon became a second-set standard, often being jammed into "The Other One."

FIRST PERFORMED: Aug. 17, 1970, at the Fillmore West in San Francisco

LAST PERFORMED: July 6, 1995, at the Riverport Amphitheater in Maryland Heights, Mo.

KEY LYRIC: "Lately it occurs to me what a long, strange trip it's been."

Bob Weir:

"There was a romance about being a young man on the road in America — it was a rite of passage. ... We had a lot of fun out on the road, got into a lot of trouble. ... We left some smoking craters of some Holiday Inns, I'll say that, and there were a lot of places that wouldn't have us back."

Truckin'

TRUCKIN' CARTOON: EVERETT COLLECTION; PEPSODENT: SCIENCE MUSEUM, LONDON, WELLCOME IMAGES/WIKI COMMONS; BOURBON ST: INFROGMATION/WIKI COMMONS

Truckin' was a dance step in the 1920s and 1930s, referred to in blues songs like Blind Boy Fuller's "Truckin' My Blues Away."

Robert Crumb was inspired by the old blues songs to draw his iconic comic "Keep On Truckin'" in 1968. Hunter refers to Crumb's comic men in the line "keep truckin' like the doo-dah man."

The Dead used a similar image on the cover of the *Europe '72* album, which featured a live, jammed-out version of "Truckin'."

Mickey Hart:

"It was autobiographical. We told our story in song. I knew that the words were strong. They were powerful, they were depicting real events in real people's lives, and they became part of the fabric, part of the history of our day. People could sing it and know there were events directly connected with it."

According to Robert Hunter, the verse about sweet Jane ("she lost her sparkle, you know she isn't the same") is a parody of a 1940s toothpaste commercial:

Poor Millicent, poor Millicent,
She never used Pepsodent
Her smile grew dim
And she lost her vim
So folks don't be like Millicent
Use Pepsodent!

Weir changed sweet Jane's fate in some versions of the song, singing: "Ever since she went and had a sex change, all her friends can say is ain't it a shame."

"Truckin'" was released as a single in an edited three-minute version and reached No. 64 on the pop singles chart, making it the Dead's most successful single until "Touch of Grey" in 1987.

A ROAD SONG

Lyricist Robert Hunter joined the band on their March 1970 tour to write them a road song. Hunter recalled, "I was on the road with the band, writing different verses in different cities, and when we were in Florida I went outside and everybody was sitting around the swimming pool. I had finally finished the lyrics, so I brought them down and the boys picked up their guitars, sat down, and wrote some rock 'n' roll changes behind it."

GARCIA REMEMBERED, "(Hunter) started going out on the road with us, coming out to see what life was like, to be able to have more of that viewpoint in his music, for the words to be more Grateful Dead words. 'Truckin'' is the result of that. ... 'Truckin'' is a song that we assembled ... it wasn't natural, and it didn't flow, and it wasn't easy, and we really labored over the bastard ... all of us together."

"Busted down on Bourbon Street" refers to the Dead's New Orleans drug bust on Jan. 31, 1970. The city narcotics squad raided the Dead's hotel after a show and arrested most of the band. The Dead didn't go back to New Orleans for 10 years.

The Players

Despite the carnival atmosphere at a live show, the members of the Grateful Dead were dedicated musicians.

PHOTOSHOT/EVERETT COLLECTION

in the band

BY MIKE DALEY

At the core of the Grateful Dead phenomenon was a group of musicians who combined a variety of backgrounds, influences and musical approaches into a one-of-a-kind mix. Writer David Gans aptly described the Grateful Dead as "America's longest running musical argument." Each member brought a unique musical sensibility to the band. As Phil Lesh wrote, "Each of us approached the music from a different direction, at angles to one another, like the spokes of a wheel." Even so, the sound of the band was one of exquisite spontaneous counterpoint, what Bob Weir called a "seamless mesh."

Despite being so associated with rock 'n' roll excess, the members of the Grateful Dead were uncommonly dedicated and serious musicians. In addition to individual practice, the band rehearsed extensively as a group from the beginning. In the early days of the Dead, daily rehearsals starting in the late mornings were the norm when the band wasn't on tour. Jerry Garcia in particular was an obsessive practicer, putting in two to three hours a day in addition to rehearsals, recordings and concerts. He was a restless explorer of the possibilities of the guitar, devouring method books in a constant quest for fresh approaches and ideas. Drummers Bill Kreutzmann and Mickey Hart would practice together for hours, apart from the rest of the band, to achieve total and intuitive synchronization. Other band members followed suit, constantly evolving and improving as musicians.

The closest thing the Dead had to a leader, JERRY GARCIA was a wildly inventive and accomplished guitar player. His distinctive, skittering, endlessly creative lead guitar most defines the sound of the Grateful Dead.

Garcia took piano lessons as a child, which gave him a background in reading musical notation. In later years, he taught himself guitar and electric bass as well as the notoriously complex and difficult pedal steel guitar. Though he rarely played it live, Garcia can be heard playing pedal steel on Dead studio cuts like "Till The Morning Comes" from *American Beauty* as well as the Crosby, Stills, Nash & Young classic "Teach Your Children."

In the early 1960s, Garcia concentrated on five-string banjo, undeterred by his missing right hand middle finger, chopped off with an axe in an accident when he was 4. By the mid-1960s he was listening to Bob Dylan and the Rolling Stones, as well as jazz saxophone visionary John Coltrane, whose complex "sheets of sound" were redefining improvisation. But Garcia's influences were extensive, and he continued throughout his life to soak in ideas from everywhere.

On early recordings of the Grateful Dead and their precursor, the Warlocks, Garcia's solos evince the vocabulary of psychedelic blues. His licks and ideas tend to be simple, though his uncommon dexterity, honed by years of dedicated practice, comes through. Garcia's playing developed noticeably over the years, becoming more complex and cerebral. His guitar work was full of rhythmic interest and invention, employing fleet scales, chromatic passing notes and arpeggios (a group of notes played one after the other). Garcia was also given to contributing terse, low string riffs, as in the intro to "China Cat Sunflower" on *Europe '72*. Strongly influenced by banjo technique, Garcia cultivated a tight, bright tone and articulation that defines his sound as much as any note choices. (If you want a taste of Garcia's brilliant banjo playing, check out the 1975 self-titled album by the bluegrass supergroup Old and in the Way.)

As a singer, Garcia tended to be more aggressive on early recordings like 1967's "Cream Puff War." On songs like "Black Peter," from 1970, his voice is much more relaxed. Garcia's voice could even take on a whispering quality, as in "Mountains of the Moon" from *Aoxomoxoa*. Over time, the rigors of touring and Garcia's substance abuse and cigarette smoking took a toll on his voice, which developed a gruffer quality and a lower range.

Strongly influenced by banjo technique, Garcia cultivated a tight, bright tone.

Jerry Garcia

GARCIA: SUSANA MILLMAN. BACKGROUND: JULIA SNEGIREVA/SHUTTERSTOCK

With a background in classical music, PHIL LESH picked up the bass guitar to join the Dead. His unique approach to the bass put the instrument on equal footing with the guitar when it came time to improvise.

Lesh's first instrument was the violin, which he started playing in the third grade before switching to the trumpet at the age of 14. According to Lesh, he was "somewhat of a prodigy" on the trumpet, playing first chair in the Young People's Symphony Orchestra and second chair in the volunteer Oakland Symphony. Lesh's musical talent was aided by the fact that he has perfect pitch (the ability to identify any pitch without reference to a musical instrument).

In 1960, Lesh gave up the trumpet and transferred to the University of California at Berkeley, where he became interested in avant-garde electronic music, especially that of German composer Karlheinz Stockhausen. Lesh was disappointed with the Berkeley music department and dropped out in his first year there. But before he left, he forged a friendship with future Dead keyboardist Tom Constanten, and the two initially bonded over their mutual interest in the music of Gustav Mahler.

After being invited to join Luciano Berio's music composition class at Mills College in Oakland in the spring of 1962, Lesh explored the music of Berio and John Cage. Lesh had stopped playing instruments altogether in 1960, but picked up the bass in 1962 to play with the Warlocks. He learned on the job, through live shows and the band's heavy rehearsal schedule.

Along with early influences Johannes Brahms and Ludwig van Beethoven, Lesh also studied the music of American iconoclast Charles Ives. Lesh has repeatedly stated how little he was inspired by other electric bass players. He has, however, cited jazz upright bassists Charles Mingus and Scott LeFaro as influences. Both musicians were known for their expansive and creative approaches to the bass, taking it beyond its traditional supportive role. For Lesh, this meant that he wanted to "play the bass in a melodic way, in a contrapuntal way, which derives ultimately from Bach."

Lesh's approach to the bass was remarkable. He rarely played the simple figures of conventional rock bass, constantly inventing new phrases. Lesh considered the entire range of the bass to be fair game, and during jams he would musically converse with the band, treating the bass as an equal and independent melody instrument. Like Jerry Garcia, he employed a variety of rhythms in his lines, often shifting unpredictably between minimal and busy playing.

Lesh was a frequent backup singer in the early years of the Dead, but rarely sang in the band after Donna Godchaux and then Brent Mydland and Vince Welnick took over the high harmonies, other than a few lead vocal appearances on "Box of Rain," "Unbroken Chain" and "Pride Of Cucamonga." Lesh's lead voice, like Bob Weir's, was best captured in the recording studio. Live, Lesh struggled to stay in pitch and also had trouble consistently singing into the microphone. From the early 1980s on, Lesh was rarely heard singing. As Weir asserted in 1977, "he blew his voice with improper singing technique."

SUSANA MILLMAN

Phil Lesh

Bob Weir

Almost entirely self-taught on guitar, BOB WEIR began to play at the age of 14. As a sufferer of dyslexia, reading music was "out of the question. My dirty little secret is that I learned by trying to imitate a piano, specifically the work of McCoy Tyner in the John Coltrane Quartet. That caught my ear and lit my flame when I was 17," he said in a 2001 interview. "I just loved what he did underneath Coltrane, so I sat with it for a long time and really tried to absorb it." Like Jerry Garcia, Weir fervently practiced the guitar, running scales and honing his rhythmic skills by playing along to a special metronome called a Trinome.

Weir has cited the Everly Brothers, Chuck Berry, the Kingston Trio and Joan Baez as early influences. He later fell under the spell of ragtime blues and gospel guitarist-singer Reverend Gary Davis, from whom he took a few lessons in the early 1970s. When he began playing with the Warlocks, Weir had been playing guitar for only three years, and his musical vocabulary was mostly limited to barre chords.

Like Garcia's leads, Weir's rhythm guitar playing evolved over the years. Weir played simpler and heavier chords in the early years of the band before he developed his spare phrasing, heavy use of partial chords and inversions and light touch. He described his role in the band as a difficult one to learn, finding his way within the Garcia-Lesh dialogue, "intuiting where the hell they're going to go and being there. It took a while to work up a touch for that." Weir occasionally took a solo, as in the version of "Friend of the Devil" that appears on *Dead Set*, and he sometimes played slide guitar (not particularly well, according to many fans), but for the most part Weir strummed chords.

Though he sang lead in the Dead from the beginning, it was not until Pigpen left the band in 1972 for health reasons that Weir took over as the strong second to Garcia. Weir's voice has a pleasant, country-tinged quality that translates particularly well in a recording studio. Live, Weir often suffered from pitch problems. Nonetheless, Weir identified singing as a priority for himself over playing the guitar. He once called singing "the most fun I know." Weir's later problems with raspiness may have been exacerbated by his penchant for exploring upper-register whoops, as he often did during the "Sunshine Daydream" coda of "Sugar Magnolia" live. He did take vocal lessons at some point to extend his range upward.

Weir evinced a particular interest in odd time signatures like 7/8, a beat pattern that he employed in his songs "Estimated Prophet," "Money Money" and "Supplication."

WEIR: SUSANA MILLMAN

Bill Kreutzmann

Drummer BILL KREUTZMANN started taking formal lessons at the age of 13. He continued to study drums privately, including lessons with Mickey Hart shortly after they first met in 1967. He calls Hart "the best drum teacher I ever had ... [he] showed me all the rudiments, and gave me really good instruction, stuff that I use every minute." Kreutzmann and Hart used unusual exercises to "entrain" synchronization. "Mickey would play a rudiment, and he would play the right arm and I would play the left. And you had to make it work," Kreutzmann said in 2011.

His early influences included Buddy Rich, Gene Krupa and Max Roach. Powerful, dynamic and absolutely solid, Kreutzmann has a subtle jazz swing in his playing. "I was born with a shuffle," he said. "I was born with a triplet. I don't know how else to say it. I just hear things, like, really relaxed."

Over time, Kreutzmann developed a style based on deep listening and interaction with the other members of the band. "I'd find myself playing, say the right hand being with Jerry, and the right foot with the bass. Each limb being with a different instrument. Maybe doing my own talking with the snare drum, but filling for the other instruments with those other limbs and breaking it up like that," he said.

Kreutzmann was "the center of the Dead, the anchor," according to Hart. From 1971 to 1974, Kreutzmann was the only drummer in the Dead. He was forced to adjust his style to fill out the sound during that time.

His drummer father moved out of the house when MICKEY HART was in grade school, and Hart began to play on the drum practice pad his dad left behind. Hart's assiduous private studies gave him a solid technical basis. Drum lessons taught him the importance of warming up, to which Hart attributes his long career.

An early influence for Hart was not musical at all — it was the sound of his hometown of Brooklyn. "I loved the rhythm of the city — I'd sit there and watch the city go by," he said in 2000. Beyond that, Hart found an interest in "the great Latin bands of the '50s — Tito Puente and Machito" and the vocalist and percussionist Babatunde Olatunji. He later took lessons from Olatunji.

In addition to the drums, Hart played an extensive variety of percussion with the Dead, including the cowbell, congas and other auxiliary percussion. There was a unique chemistry between Bill Kreutzmann and Hart — a communication that to Hart was "telepathic ... a secret language that we cannot describe." An unusual aspect of Hart's style is that he typically uses mallets, contrasting with Kreutzmann's use of sticks, which Hart, with a wink, described as "archaic."

Mickey Hart

KREUTZMANN: WIKI COMMONS, HART: SUSANA MILLMAN

Born Ron McKernan, PIGPEN was a completely self-taught musician. Though he is best known as a singer, harmonica player and organist, he also played standard and bottleneck slide guitar. His acoustic guitar playing can be heard on "Katie Mae" from the Dead's live album *History of the Grateful Dead Vol. 1 (Bear's Choice)*. Pigpen learned much of his blues guitar vocabulary from Jerry Garcia — they met in 1961 and Garcia showed Pig guitar chords and licks. He was also learning the harmonica on his own and cultivating a singing style strongly influenced by Sam "Lightnin'" Hopkins. "I began singin' at 16. I wasn't in school; I was just goofin'. I've always been singing along with records — my dad was a disc jockey, and it's been what I wanted to do," he said.

Pigpen's father was a boogie-woogie pianist and R&B disc jockey on Berkeley radio in the early 1950s. The younger McKernan absorbed the music from his father's large collection of records and became interested in down-home blues. As Garcia commented about Pigpen, "His thing is blues, almost nothing but blues. He's got some interest in other kinds of music, but it's mostly blues."

Pigpen's role within the Dead was primarily that of an organist playing functional chords and riffs. He also played piano on several shows during the Dead's 1970 summer tour. He was not a keyboard soloist, but was adept on the harmonica and as a blues vocalist. "He could improvise lyrics endlessly; that was his real forte," Jerry Garcia once commented.

Pigpen also sometimes contributed congas and tambourine to the Dead's percussion texture. According to onetime Dead manager Jon McIntyre, Pigpen's keyboard playing declined as a result of his alcoholism. He told interviewer Blair Jackson, "In the beginning it was really imaginative and the tempos were good, and then, after a while, after a certain number of years, it got into that maudlin space where it was just not good playing. The timing was off."

Pigpen's role in the band changed over the years. In their Warlock days, Pig was the dominant lead singer of the band, with a big voice and a professional delivery. His role diminished after 1968 or so, and he doesn't even appear on the 1969 album *Aoxomoxoa*. Nonetheless, Pigpen was a big part of the Dead's live shows through 1971, when he took ill with the cirrhosis that would end his life at the age of 27.

Pigpen's role within the Dead was primarily that of an organist.

Pigpen

PHOTOSHOT/EVERETT COLLECTION

Tom Constanten

Keyboardist TOM CONSTANTEN took piano lessons as a child, and, like Lesh, studied composition formally with Luciano Berio at Mills College in Oakland. Influenced by John Cage, Constanten composed for "prepared piano," in which a variety of objects, like pencils and small pieces of metal, were stuffed between piano strings to yield an unusual and percussive sound.

Back home in Las Vegas, Constanten performed his own compositions in piano recitals and had his orchestral work premiered with the Las Vegas Civic Orchestra and University of Nevada Orchestra and Chorus. When he joined the Dead as a second keyboardist in 1968 — supplementing the contributions of Pigpen — Constanten had already worked with Phil Lesh in a series of concerts at the San Francisco Mime Troupe in May 1964. In fact, Constanten and Lesh had been fast friends and roommates since meeting at Mills College in 1962.

As a classical pianist, Constanten struggled with the stage keyboard technology of the time, which relegated him to electric organs. As he later recounted, "I couldn't find a place for the sustained sound of an organ in a guitar band context — ahhh, for a piano!" Onstage, he could barely hear the organ over Garcia's electric guitar. When his lines do emerge on live recordings of Dead jams in songs like "The Eleven," they are deftly played strings of eighth notes, Bach-like in their snaking invention.

Constanten was most comfortable with the Dead in a studio environment, where he could control the sound levels. He came into his own as the keyboardist on much of *Aoxomoxoa*. His contributions on piano and celeste (a chiming piano-like instrument) on the studio version of "St. Stephen" are essential. He left the band in 1970.

Bruce Hornsby

Never an official member of the band, BRUCE HORNSBY frequently played with the Dead from 1990 to 1992. After an abortive year of piano lessons at the age of 7, he didn't start playing the keyboard until he was about 17 years old. Later he played by ear, learning songs off of records. He eventually attended the University of Miami and the Berklee College of Music in Boston, which gave him the strong technical basis that informed his rapid-fire runs and arpeggios. His distinctive, if somewhat uniform, piano style was made famous in his hit solo records "The Way It Is" and "Mandolin Rain." His contributions added a rippling undercurrent to the Dead's live performances, and he was a fan favorite. Hornsby also contributed accordion to some Dead shows, especially during guest slots before and after his regular 1990-92 tenure.

PHOTOS: SUSANA MILLMAN

Brent Mydland

Mydland was with the Dead longer than any other keyboardist.

The Dead's fourth keyboardist (after Pigpen, Tom Constanten and Keith Godchaux) was BRENT MYDLAND, who started piano lessons at age 6 and had formal lessons through his junior year in high school. As he later commented, "My sister took lessons and it looked fun to me, so I did too. There was always a piano around the house and I wanted to play it. When I couldn't play it I would beat on it anyway."

His mother insisted that Mydland practice his music for two hours each day. He also played trumpet up to his last year of high school. He originally aspired to be "a high school band teacher or something. I played trumpet in the [marching] band ... then my senior year I got kicked out of the band for having long hair ... so that was the end of my band career. I gave up the trumpet and concentrated on the keyboards."

Mydland was with the Dead from 1979 until his death in 1990, longer than any other keyboardist. He easily fit into the band's sound and added his own contributions, such as in *Go to Heaven*, which featured two of Mydland's songs, "Far From Me" and "Easy to Love You," the latter written with Weir collaborator John Perry Barlow. On the Dead's next album, *In the Dark*, Mydland co-wrote the fan favorite "Hell in a Bucket" with Weir and Barlow as well as the song "Tons of Steel." His high, gravelly vocal harmonies and heartfelt leads greatly added to the band's vocal mix. Mydland played several different electric pianos and synthesizers throughout his tenure, as well as the Hammond B-3 organ.

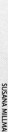SUSANA MILLMAN

As a longtime member of the San Francisco-based popular theater rock band the Tubes, VINCE WELNICK learned on the job through countless rehearsals and gigs. When he joined the Dead in 1990 after the death of Brent Mydland, he was adept at piano, organ and synthesizer. With the Dead, Welnick tended to gravitate toward the synth and organ when Bruce Hornsby was playing second keyboards. As Welnick commented, "when Bruce is around, I leave the piano work to him."

Welnick's reliance on synthesized sounds rather than the more traditional piano, electric piano and organ of his predecessors has led to divided opinions among Deadheads about Welnick's contributions. Some fans have commented that he was less given to exploration than the other members of the band, preferring to stick to the basic musical themes. Welnick's ability to sing the high vocal harmonies required for the Dead's arrangements contributed to his utility in the band. He was an occasional lead singer with the band as well, contributing a lead vocal to "Way to Go Home" and a verse to the Dead's version of Bob Dylan's "Maggie's Farm."

SUSANA MILLMAN

Vince Welnick

Keith Godchaux

His father had worked as a pianist and a singer, and KEITH GODCHAUX started piano lessons at age 5. Godchaux had five years of classical training, but "I didn't have the temperament to pursue it," he said in an interview. He had a solid technical basis from years of study and practice, but, as he commented, "it wasn't deep; none of it stuck."

Godchaux joined the band in September 1971, just as Pigpen entered the hospital with cirrhosis of the liver. Like his predecessor Tom Constanten, Keith came into the band with little rock 'n' roll experience. As he said in 1976, "I'm just now starting to learn about the type of music I'm playing now. ... I never played rock 'n' roll before I started playing with the Grateful Dead."

In spite of his humble self-assessment, Godchaux fit in well, according to Phil Lesh, "He was so brilliant at the beginning. That guy had it all, he could play anything. ... It's like he came forth fully grown. He didn't have to work his way into it."

Though he started out with the band playing piano and organ fairly equally, by the end of his first tour with he was playing acoustic piano almost exclusively. In the middle of 1973 he added a Fender Rhodes electric piano and then switched exclusively to electric piano in 1977 after a brief flirtation with synthesizers.

Initially, Godchaux's melodic, fluid style perfectly complemented the Dead's improvisatory approach. Following the group's mid '70s hiatus, he simplified his playing and increasingly emulated Garcia's guitar lines. Lesh later wrote that by 1978, "Keith's playing had degenerated to the point that most of us were simply trying to lose him onstage ... never a paragon of self-esteem, Keith's increasing drug and alcohol use had put him in an almost vegetative state. His musical timing was suffering, and he had developed some annoying habits onstage, notably slavish imitation of Jerry's lead lines, a tic that began to irritate Jerry to no end."

EVERETT COLLECTION

ROGER GUPTA/WIKI COMMONS

Growing up in Muscle Shoals, Ala., DONNA JEAN GODCHAUX learned to sing by ear and by trial and error. As part of the vocal group Southern Comfort, she worked as a backup singer at the famed Muscle Shoals studio, recording with Elvis Presley, Ben E. King, Joe Tex and on Percy Sledge's "When a Man Loves a Woman." Godchaux sang with the Grateful Dead from 1972 to 1979, while her husband Keith played keyboards, lending her voice to harmonies and occasional lead vocals, as on "Sunrise" and the bridge to "The Music Never Stopped."

She remains a contentious topic with Deadheads. There is no doubt that Godchaux often suffered from vocal problems onstage, her voice sometimes drifting flat in pitch or taking on a harsh rasp as the rigors of the road took their toll. As she told *Rolling Stone* in 2014, "I was a studio singer, never singing off-key. I was used to having headphones and being in a controlled environment. Then, all of a sudden, I went to being onstage with the Dead. ... Everything was so loud onstage. And not to mention being inebriated. I can't defend myself very much, but I can't blame it all on that." ●

She remains a contentious topic with Deadheads.

Donna Jean Godchaux

FLEA CIRCUS: DPA, FRANK LEONHARDT/FILEAP PHOTO. EMILY DICKINSON: WIKI COMMONS

Workingman's Dead
1970

SONG WRITTEN BY: Jerry Garcia; lyrics by Robert Hunter

VOCALS: Jerry Garcia, Bob Weir and Phil Lesh

PERFORMED 338 TIMES. First played in November '69, it was initially an instrumental jam inside tunes like "Dark Star." It was played inside many "Playing in the Band" jams, starting in 1973. It went on hiatus several times, including for two years in '78-'79.

FIRST PERFORMED WITH LYRICS: Dec. 4, 1969, at the Fillmore West in San Francisco

LAST PERFORMED: June 28, 1995, at the Palace in Auburn Hills, Mich.

KEY LYRIC: "What I want to know is, are you kind?"

FINDING UNCLE JOHN

There have been many theories about the identity of Uncle John. One candidate is John Cohen of the New Lost City Ramblers — his nickname was Uncle John, and Garcia was a fan of the band and went to see them often. Cohen himself wondered if the song was about the Ramblers, and noticed that several of their songs are mentioned in the lyrics. These include "Buck Dancer's Choice" and "The Story the Crow Told Me."

. . . .

Another possibility is Jerry Garcia himself — his full name is Jerome John Garcia.

. . . .

Lyricist Robert Hunter claimed that "Uncle John was a Kansas City drifter who had a flea circus, little critters in band uniforms with instruments you could see under a magnifying glass. They didn't actually play them, but if they had, what a tiny music that tiny music would be."

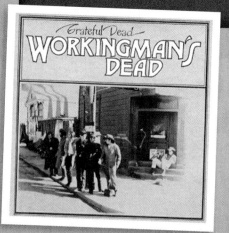

"Ain't no time to hate" may refer to an Emily Dickinson poem:
*"I had no time to hate, because
The grave would hinder me
And life was not so ample I
Could finish enmity."*

Uncle John's

TOP: PHOTO BY RAY STEVENSON/REX USA/EVERETT COLLECTION. BOTTOM: EDMUND J. SULLIVAN RUBAIYAT/WIKI COMMONS

The CSN Connection

The Dead credited Crosby, Stills & Nash for inspiring the harmonies on "Uncle John's Band." The two bands spent a lot of time together in 1969 and 1970. David Crosby said, "They had listened to us a lot … but we never sat down with them in a room and said, 'Okay now, you sing this, you sing this.' That never happened. Those guys are brilliant. They knew exactly what they were doing, and they evolved their own version of it. They just credited us to be nice." Crosby, Stills & Nash have returned the favor by performing the song live.

"Uncle John's Band" was released as a single in an edited version that removed the word "goddamn." It reached No. 69 in the pop singles chart, making it the Dead's first top 100 single.

GARCIA DIDN'T LIKE THE SINGLE: "I gave them instructions on how to properly edit it and they garbled it so completely … what an atrocity!"

FROM *ROLLING STONE*'S 1970 REVIEW: "Staunch Dead freaks probably will hate this song. It's done acoustically for a starter. No Garcia leads. No smasho drumming. In fact, it's got a mariachi/calypso type feeling. … It's really very pretty. … Just listen to it, and try not to smile."

Jerry Garcia:

"I was listening to records of the Bulgarian Women's Choir and also this Greek-Macedonian music, these penny whistlers, and on one of those records there was this little turn of melody that was so lovely that I thought, 'Gee, if I could get this into a song it would be so great.' So I stole it! Actually, I took a little piece of the melody, so I can't say I plagiarized the whole thing. Of course it became so transmogrified when Phil and Bob added their harmony parts to it that it really was no longer the part of the song that was special for me."

Band

"Like the morning sun you come and like the wind you go" may allude to a line from the *Rubaiyat of Omar Khayyam*: "I came like water and like wind I go." The famous skull-and-roses image that adorns the Grateful Dead's self-titled 1971 live album comes from a 19th-century illustration for the *Rubaiyat*, which is a collection of Persian poems translated by Edward FitzGerald.

ROCK AND ROLL HALL OF FAME AND MUSEUM/AP PHOTO

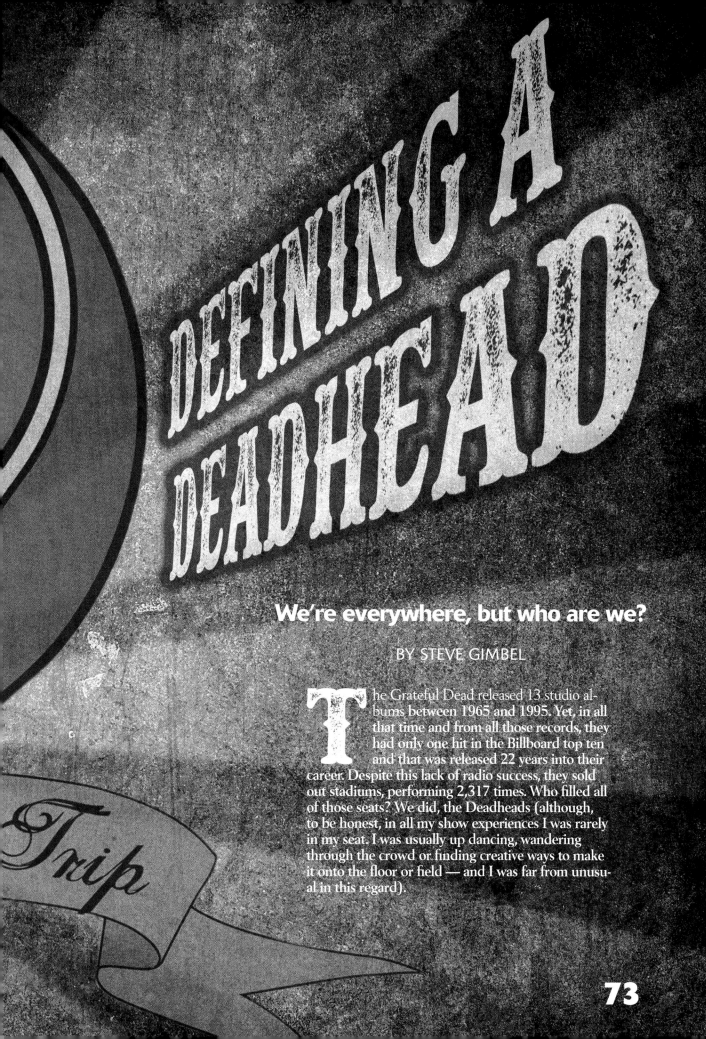

DEFINING A DEADHEAD

We're everywhere, but who are we?

BY STEVE GIMBEL

The Grateful Dead released 13 studio albums between 1965 and 1995. Yet, in all that time and from all those records, they had only one hit in the Billboard top ten and that was released 22 years into their career. Despite this lack of radio success, they sold out stadiums, performing 2,317 times. Who filled all of those seats? We did, the Deadheads (although, to be honest, in all my show experiences I was rarely in my seat. I was usually up dancing, wandering through the crowd or finding creative ways to make it onto the floor or field — and I was far from unusual in this regard).

Deadheads are known for creatively modifying their VW buses.

Deadheads say with pride, "We are everywhere." Indeed, your auto mechanic, the guy working in the health food store, your college professor, your heart surgeon, your rabbi, even your United States senator might be a Deadhead. But what does it mean to be a Deadhead? Could you be a Deadhead and not realize it? If you were born after Jerry Garcia died, is there any way you can still become a Deadhead?

It's All About the Music

The simplest account of what it means to be a Deadhead comes from the host of the syndicated weekly *Grateful Dead Hour*, David Gans. When asked what makes someone a Deadhead, Gans responded, "Loving the music is the only criterion."

Of course, there's lots of great music out there. Loving the music of the Grateful Dead is different. Before there were dedicated Dead stations on satellite radio, Dead songs were rarely found on the airwaves. Even when a Dead song was played, it was usually a studio track, not the expansive, exploratory jams that truly captured the imaginations of Deadheads.

Generally someone had to invite you on the

bus, a friend who was already there — someone who had bootlegs to play and who knew what he or she was listening to. For me, it was my friend Larry playing tapes he got from his older brother Jay in his basement. To some, the music sounds like aimless noodling, but for others — those destined to become Deadheads — there is something profound in the band's extended improvisations.

Deadheads truly love the music. Perhaps the only thing longer than a late '60s "Dark Star" is the conversation Deadheads can have about it. Before the Internet made the information so much easier to access, countless hours were spent by Deadheads paging through set lists in spiral-bound editions of *Deadbase*, a rigorously researched, informally published and periodically updated collection of the songs performed at each concert, with the date, location and personnel noted.

A Culture of Sharing

Nowadays, the music is easy to find. There are scads of Grateful Dead CDs, not only the original albums but newer, beautifully produced live shows from the original soundboard recordings. Websites give Dead fans instant access to mul-

EVERETT COLLECTION

It's never too late to be a Deadhead; fans come from all walks of life, and share an abiding love for the music.

PHOTOS: SUSANA MILLMAN

tiple bootlegged versions of virtually any show. But for decades, the music was largely underground. Sharing it served to form bonds among Deadheads. Every Deadhead had a collection of cassette tapes, each with a set from a different show. These were the currency of the Deadhead community. When you met new Deadheads, finding your way into their circle of fellow travelers, you would run down the list of tapes you had and your new acquaintances would do the same. When you had a tape they did not, you would gladly copy it for them.

While the tapes were the coin of the realm, actual money was never exchanged. Sharing your tapes was a central part of being a Deadhead. You allowed a fellow fan to appreciate a wider range of the Dead's work while also becoming a part of their Deadhead life.

To be offered tapes was a rite of acceptance. It meant that you were being welcomed into this new circle of Heads. Your connection with the community was widened, as was your

Deadheads prize personal expression.

Before file sharing and online archives, Deadheads got together and shared their favorite recordings of live Dead shows.

collection. You now had another set, completing a show, filling in a gap in a particular tour or opening you up to a different phase of the band.

When putting together a stereo system, a Deadhead made certain to get a dual tape deck to assure the quality of the reproduced shows. Inside the clear plastic case that held the cassette, you carefully listed the songs — noting with an arrow which ones led seamlessly into others — and identified the venue of the show, the date and whether the tape was of the first or second set. You added some art or flourishes and left your name on the inside so that your connection with this Deadhead brother or sister would remain every time the tape was played. Your own collection of tapes displayed the multitude of handwritings and styles of those Deadheads you had met on your path. Before social media, a tape collection was a Deadhead friend list.

The Elements of Deadhead Culture

Like all other communities, Deadheads developed their own set of icons and rituals and a specific language. Iconic images include dancing bears, skeletons and roses, and perhaps most well-known, the stealie, the schematic topview of a skull with a lightning bolt or some other symbol in the circle denoting the brain cavity.

Tie-dyed clothing is now seen everywhere, but it used to clearly indicate a Deadhead. The association of tie dye with the band goes back to its beginnings when, in order to make ends meet in the band's communal house, the members' girlfriends would tie dye clothing to be sold at a local consignment shop. Tie-dyed clothes were readily available for purchase on Shakedown Street, the impromptu marketplace

that would appear in the parking lot outside of every show. Some of these were handmade by artisans. Others had clever slogans or intricate pictures silkscreened onto them.

Being a part of the Deadhead community was not merely to be influenced by the band and its music. The influence went the other way as well. The Deadheads helped make Dead music what it was. According to guitarist Bob Weir, "The music originates in the azimuth, the space between the band and the audience. The band is on the stage and the audience is in the seats, but between those two is the azimuth where they meet and that is the source of the music." The music is in the Deadheads and the Deadheads are in the music.

Because the music was a happening, a reflection of the where, when and who of a specific place and time, each show was unique. Dedicated fans wanted to be a part of as many of these occurrences as possible. The result was touring. Unlike most music fans, Deadheads did not wait for the band to come to them; rather, they followed the band.

Different venues had completely different feels. Indoor shows at Madison Square Garden in New York City had a metropolitan energy, whereas those at Hampton Coliseum in Virginia had a coziness — it felt like you were seeing the band in a high school gymnasium. Outdoor venues where you could dance on grass or in dirt, such as at Deer Creek in Indiana, Buckeye Lake in Ohio, Red Rocks in Colorado or Meriwether Post Pavilion in Maryland, gave a sense of openness and organic flow to the shows. At stadiums like Soldier Field in Chicago you were lost in a sea of Deadheads. The different energies of the locations showed up in the music — some shows

SUSANA MILLMAN

DEADHEAD CREATIVITY

While the artistry of the Grateful Dead on stage is what brought Deadheads together, the community encouraged creativity from everyone. This was expressed in myriad ways.

Tickets for shows could be bought directly from the band, allowing Deadheads to bypass the commercial ticket dealers. The process involved sending an index card of a specific size with particular information in exact spots on the card. Deviation from form could mean no tickets, so the rules were followed exactly. But such restrictions led to a need to express creativity, and this led to meticulously filled-in cards sent in uniquely decorated envelopes featuring colorful hand-drawn masterpieces.

Shakedown Street, the marketplace in the parking lot, featured stickers, T-shirts and all sorts of wares for the concertgoer to purchase. Because there were so many vendors, goods had to be eye-catching. Bright colors and intricate designs competed with creative slogans that often got chuckles. Corporate logos might be transformed into Dead references or straight cultural references might be tweaked with a clever twist. The parking lot was a cornucopia of art and wit.

The vehicles in the parking lot were another medium for Deadhead creativity. Cars often were adorned with multiple bumper stickers, and vans and VW microbuses were painted in bright colors. These were traveling homes, and Deadheads showed themselves to be talented exterior decorators.

Right: On Shakedown Street, Tourheads could support their Dead habit with tie-dyed T-shirt sales.

The Grateful dead inspired an army of loyal fans to follow them around the country during their heavy tour schedule.

PHOTOS: SUSANA MILLMAN

more frenetic, others more mellow, some of them giddy and goofy, others with an edge.

No matter the place and no matter the tenor of the music, at the end of the show you could hug the equally sweaty person next to you who shared the experience. One of the great bonding moments between Deadheads today is finding the shows that you both attended. You may not have seen each other there, but your lines through space and time intersected.

Deadhead Status

One result of the culture of traveling with the Dead was the establishment

TOP: PETER BROOKER/REX USA/EVERETT COLLECTION; BOTTOM: WIKI COMMONS

of a sort of class status within the Deadhead community based upon the shows you had seen. Deadhead credibility could be earned in several ways. The standard measure was the number of shows. The more concerts you had attended, the more authentic you could claim to be. Another route to legitimacy was to see a significant number of consecutive shows. To tour, that is, to see all the concerts on a particular spring, summer or fall run, gained you major cache.

The date of your first show mattered. Deadheads refer to this as when you "got on the bus." The earlier your first show, the greater your status. In the late 1980s, it was an insult to be called a Touch-head. "Touch of Grey" from the 1987 release *In the Dark* was a surprise radio hit. Its popularity caused attendance at shows to balloon. To be a Touch-head was to be a mere bandwagon fan, not a true Deadhead.

Finally, one's bona fides could be estab-

lished by having seen a notable show. It could have been a particularly good performance. Some shows were magic in that the band was particularly on that night. A noteworthy show could connect with a significant event in the band's history: The first time Bruce Hornsby sat in on accordion, or the show that gave Jerry heat stroke. A show might be note-worthy because of the debut of a new song or what Deadheads call a breakout, when a song that had not been performed in a long time made its reappearance.

I was fortunate to be in the Capital Centre in Landover, Md., on Sept. 3, 1988, when, at the end of what was otherwise a pretty nondescript show, Garcia shocked everyone by launching into "Ripple," which the band had not played electrically in 17 years and never would again. It was like hitting the Deadhead lottery. Those of us who were there not only had the treat of experi-encing it, but also won special Deadhead cred.

Deadheads express themselves and their love for the band on all kinds of canvases, including concrete.

PETER BROOKER/REX USA/EVERETT COLLECTION

Can You Still Become a Deadhead?

What about the new crop of Dead fans? We still have Furthur, Phil and Friends, RatDog and Dark Star Orchestra. Does attending these shows count? If you were born after Jerry Garcia died in 1995, are the doors to the Deadhead community closed?

David Dodd, author of *The Annotated Grateful Dead Lyrics* and the person who got "Deadhead" included as an official subject heading in the Library of Congress, despises any exclusivity. "I've had this question from a number of younger people who never saw the band, but have come to love the music, and actually write to me to ask if they could be Deadheads if they never experienced the Grateful Dead live. I've always replied to them that of course they can claim the designation — it's entirely a matter of self-identification! I've never bought into that 'more Deadhead than thou' thing. ... Do you love the music? Does it make you happy when it plays, and can you not get enough of it? Then you are a Deadhead."

But is there a threshold? When do you go from just liking the music to being a full-on Deadhead? Nicholas Meriwether, director of the Grateful Dead Archive at the University of California, Santa Cruz and author of *All Graceful Instruments: The Contexts of the Grateful Dead Phenomenon*, contends that it is a question of using the Grateful Dead as a lens to make sense of the world.

"We live in a world in which Ann Coulter calls herself a Deadhead, and I also remember a weird letter-to-the-editor exchange in *Golden Road* in which Republican Deadheads were defending their position. I do think an ethos, if not a worldview or philosophy, inheres in the music, lyrics and scene; and I think that those derive from a fundamental sense of taking meaning from, and deriving an outlook on life from, the music."

Unlike other bands that originated in the same place at the same time, groups like Jefferson Airplane or Country Joe and the Fish, the Dead's music was never intended to convey a message.

The Grateful Dead dancing bears appear on the back cover of *History of the Grateful Dead, Volume One (Bear's Choice), and* are a tribute to Owsley "Bear" Stanley, who recorded and produced the album.

ALEX MILAN TRACY/SIPA USA/AP IMAGES

SUSANA MILLMAN

It did not have a point of view you were to take away. The band was not telling you what to think or how to feel. Rather, the music was designed as a happening, an event connecting the members of the band with the audience, open and different every time, something that was personal.

The Grateful Dead were and are a surviving vestige of 1960s counterculture that sought freedom from traditional expectations by creating an environment where everyone was free to experiment with their own sense of being while still belonging to a community. Deadheads are those who come together in the shadow of the Grateful Dead to keep that goal alive.

As Rosie McGee, photographer and author of *Dancing with the Dead: A Photographic Memoir* and former longtime partner of bassist Phil Lesh puts it, "Deadheads deeply love and identify with the Grateful Dead — the band,

the music, the history, the graphic icons, the traveling lifestyle and the community they belong to (of kind and likeminded folks) that has grown to astounding numbers over the last fifty years.

"Over two million Deadheads worldwide have manifested their Deadhead-ness in unique ways that fit their age, upbringing, financial means and level of fervor. But while the cliché Deadhead description involves the wearing of tie-dyed gypsy clothing and long hair, the taking of psychedelics and the smoking of weed and a tendency to express themselves by quoting Grateful Dead song lyrics — that's not the whole picture. Aged from twelve to ninety, Deadheads are also found in many walks of life that require them to conceal their true identities, until going to a Dead-centric event cuts them loose to be themselves." ●

The Grateful Dead always encouraged fans to dance at their shows, and part of getting into the groove meant getting out of your seat to *move*.

The Visionary
Dead

The Grateful Dead were prophets of a new business model.

BY SUSAN BALTER-REITZ

One of the great mysteries that surround the Grateful Dead is how the legacy of a seemingly ragtag bunch of musicians has survived, even thrived, 20 years after the last Dead concert. Decisions made during the height of the group's fame ensured that decades after Jerry Garcia's death, the Dead would have a lively presence in the digital world. In fact, the Dead, who share Northern California roots with many digital pioneers, embraced the ethos of the Internet age even before anyone knew what that was — from sharing to connecting to innovating. The Dead were digital before digital was digital.

AP PHOTO/GUY PALMIOTTO. BACKGROUND: DRHITCH/SHUTTERSTOCK

Reliving the Concerts

The Dead were way ahead of their time, allowing fans to make recordings of live shows and trade tapes among themselves — as long as no money changed hands.

Unlike most musical groups of their time, the Grateful Dead were primarily a touring band. Being a Grateful Dead fan was about seeing a show; each performance had a unique set list and idiosyncratic performances. The Dead would often play multiple nights in the same venue, rarely repeating a song.

Early in the Dead's touring career, fans began taping shows so that they could relive the experience. Tapes were a gateway to the Grateful Dead; many fans were turned on by tapes from friends. *Relix* magazine was founded in 1974 as a way to connect Grateful Dead tapers, and it was soon followed by *Dupree's Diamond News* and *Golden Road*. These publications created a community of tapers and tape collectors who not only traded with each other, but also seeded the fan community with their recordings and went out of their way to share the music. This spirit of generosity presaged the Internet's sharing culture; for the cost of a tape and postage, fans who could not record shows were able to access the music.

The Dead weren't focused on radio airplay and promoting albums. The band was about like-minded people finding each other and sharing music. Although not officially sanctioned until 1984, the Dead tolerated fans distributing their music as long as no one profited from the tapes of the shows. It was fine to trade or give away recordings, but selling shows was verboten. Jerry Garcia famously (and perhaps legendarily) opined, "Once we're done with it, the audience can have it," referring to the fans' practice of taping and trading shows. Of course, Garcia was a taper himself. Before he formed the Grateful Dead he followed and taped Bill Monroe.

Cassette tapes, state of the art in the '70s, gave way to DATs (digital audio tapes) by the early '90s. While DAT technology was never mainstream in the United States, Grateful Dead tapers quickly adopted the digital equipment. The audiophiles who spent untold dollars and hours taping shows have left a legacy of music easily accessible to anyone with a browser.

The zealous devotion of the Grateful Dead to the quality of the sound also secured the durability of the music into the digital age. Exceptional sound engineers were drawn into the band's nexus early on. Owsley "Bear" Stanley was the group's first soundman. His passion was extraordinary sound; his early influence on the band led to two important outcomes. First, he

SUSANA MILLMAN

PHOTOS: JEFF CHIU/AP PHOTO

A Countercultural Archive

The Grateful Dead Archive, hosted at UC Santa Cruz, provides a rich and well-organized selection of visual and media artifacts. Dead Central, the physical archive located in the McHenry Library, is a mecca for anyone interested in the Grateful Dead. For those who can't make the trek, the online archive provides a similar state of wonder. In keeping with the essence of the Grateful Dead, the archive invites fans to submit their own digital artifacts.

was constantly experimenting with the best equipment he could find, including innovative ways to capture live shows. Second, Bear recorded every Grateful Dead show he worked on. He wanted to create a "sonic journal" in order to improve his soundboard mix for the next show. The sound engineers who followed Bear had the same dedication to providing and capturing the best concert experience possible. The result is that the band has a nearly complete archive of its shows, with stunning quality and mix.

Archive.org, a nonprofit founded in 1996 to preserve the history of the digital world, was a natural landing pad for the tapers who had converted their music to digital files. The Grateful Dead was one of the earliest bands to allow their music to be uploaded to the live music archive. Nearly 10,000 Dead recordings are available at archive.org for streaming or download, including almost every concert the band ever performed. Most concerts have been recorded by multiple sources and the recordings display different characteristics depending on where the taper was located at a concert venue. These recordings, for the most part, have been painstakingly mastered to ensure the best possible quality. Some of the early shows are rather rough sounding. The very first recording at archive.org was caught by microphones scattered around an Acid Test and preserves the ethos of experimentation that birthed the band.

The web is rife with opportunities to see and hear the band. YouTube is loaded with videos of everything from full concerts to fan-made videos. GDradio.net is a streaming service that plays live shows and syndicated radio programs, including David Gans' "Grateful Dead Hour."

Top: In April 2008, Mickey Hart (left) and Bob Weir, along with other surviving members of the Grateful Dead, decided to donate their archives to the University of California at Santa Cruz.

Bottom: UCSC Chancellor George Blumenthal holds up a tie and shirts given to him by the Grateful Dead.

The tape culture that grew up around the Grateful Dead has kept alive their music in ways no one could have anticipated.

SUSANA MILLMAN

The Dead on the Early Net

Even before the Grateful Dead disbanded in 1995, fans were using tools such as USENET and ARPANET to connect and converse. In the late '80s and early '90s, The WELL was a thriving bulletin board where Dead fans would discuss recent concerts and upcoming tours. Two popular listservs, net.music.gdead, which started in the early '80s, and netlist@gdead.berkeley.edu, encouraged discussions about the band. Although very few people were on the Internet in these pre-browser days, Deadheads had already found each other and were using the Internet to share tapes, debate and discuss.

A Community and Culture

"Dead freaks unite." This simple invitation, issued on the band's 1971 album *Grateful Dead*, spurred a dedicated following unknown in the history of rock 'n' roll. Although its purpose was to gather names for a newsletter, the solicitation was read by fans as an act of community. The newsletter was published through 1980, when it was replaced by the "Grateful Dead Almanac," a slicker publication that often included original art and poetry. This version of the newsletter continued publication even after the retirement of the Grateful Dead in 1995. Receiving the "Almanac" in the mail was like hearing from a long-lost friend.

In 2011, the "Almanac" went entirely digital, distributed on dead.net, the official website of the Grateful Dead. In the introduction to the almanac's new format, the editors noted that "a big part of the Grateful Dead legacy has always been about looking forward, being open to innovation, new technologies, etc." Dead.net is an important resource for the expanding community of Deadheads.

Social media provides instant updates and the chance for fans to share the Grateful Dead experience. Twitter's #gratefuldead uncovers an alluring potpourri of images, musings, music, links and news — old and new — about the band. Social media keeps veteran Deadheads plugged in while allowing newbies to quickly find the scene.

All this new media chatter is founded on the dynamics that emerged between Deadheads during the band's touring career. To be a Deadhead is to want to talk about the Dead — to engage in analyses of shows, to plan the next trip, to think about the world of music and art more broadly. The Deadhead family was shaped by the communal experience of a concert and reinforced by the warm feelings that continued long after a show. In the digital age, the Dead family is just a few clicks away. ●

COLLECTIBLE CONCERT IMAGES
FROM THE '80s ON

Susana Millman Photography
mamarazi@mac.com
http://www.mamarazi.com
1 (415) 282-0609

AP PHOTO

Beyond

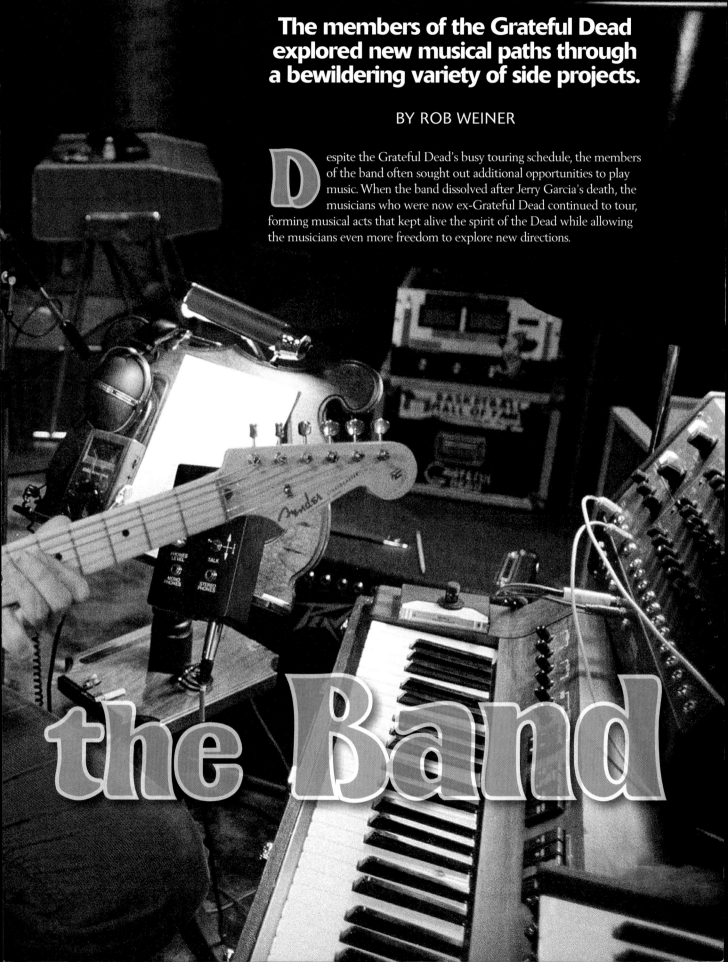

The members of the Grateful Dead explored new musical paths through a bewildering variety of side projects.

BY ROB WEINER

Despite the Grateful Dead's busy touring schedule, the members of the band often sought out additional opportunities to play music. When the band dissolved after Jerry Garcia's death, the musicians who were now ex-Grateful Dead continued to tour, forming musical acts that kept alive the spirit of the Dead while allowing the musicians even more freedom to explore new directions.

the Band

caption

Garcia: Versatile and Various

The closest thing the Dead had to a leader, Jerry Garcia was a prolific and versatile musician. He was always willing to lend a hand to friends on their studio recordings and played live with many different bands. It didn't matter what style of music. Garcia, either on his own or with others, played jazz, bluegrass, country, folk, avant garde noise punk, pop, gospel, traditional rock, world music and hard rock. One of his earliest guest appearances was on Jefferson Airplane's 1967 masterpiece *Surrealistic Pillow*, where he is credited as being a "musical and spiritual advisor." His most bizarre guest appearance was on one track (with Mickey Hart) for noise artist Negativland on 1987's *Escape from Noise*. His list of guest appearances is so vast that it would take up this whole article, but a few of the artists Garcia worked with include the Neville Brothers, David Crosby, Ornette Coleman, Warren Zevon, Country Joe, Jefferson Starship and Sanjay Mishra.

In 1971, Garcia released the jazz-infused instrumental album *Hooteroll?* with keyboardist Howard Wales while also performing on country rock outfit the New Rider's of the Purple Sage's self-titled debut (Garcia was a full band member and played pedal steel). Warner Brothers released Garcia's first proper solo album, *Garcia*, in 1972, with songs by lyricist Robert Hunter and drums by Bill Kreutzmann. In 1974, Garcia released his second solo album, *Compliments of Garcia*, on the band's short-lived label for solo releases, Round Records. In 1975, one of the most important albums from a Garcia side project, *Old and in the Way*, from a bluegrass band of the same name, was released. Garcia played banjo on that album, which is the biggest-sell-

ALBUM SPOTLIGHT

The Very Best of Jerry Garcia

For those who want a taste of nearly everything that Garcia did outside of the Grateful Dead, look no further. The first disc in this collection has standout album tracks from various Garcia-related studio releases, including tunes like "Deal," "Loser" and "Sugaree" that are also Dead staples. The second disc features live tracks, with highlights including the lovely "Catfish John" from Old and in the Way; "Ripple" and "Deep Elem Blues" from the Jerry Garcia Acoustic Band; and a spirited cover of Los Lobos' "Evangeline" and several Bob Dylan covers from the Jerry Garcia Band. A standout track is a jazzy cover of the Beatles' "Dear Prudence" from the short-lived band Reconstruction. Here's hoping that the Garcia estate sees fit to release a complete Reconstruction show in the near future.

LEFT: SUSANA MILLMAN; RIGHT: NORTHFOTO/SHUTTERSTOCK

ing bluegrass record in history. The album still crackles with energy.

Garcia would go on to release many other non-Grateful Dead albums, and he developed a sort of second musical family, including mandolinist David Grisman, bass player John Kahn (who performed with every one of Garcia's side projects) and keyboardist Merl Saunders, who collaborated with Garcia throughout the '70s. Garcia and Saunders released albums as Legion of Mary and Reconstruction, as well as under their own names.

Garcia's longest-lasting side project was the Jerry Garcia Band, which he led from the mid-'70s up to his death. The Jerry Garcia Band included a rotating cast of top-notch musicians, including keyboardist Nicky Hopkins, Grateful Dead bandmates Keith and Donna Godchaux and keyboardist Melvin Seals.

The 1980s and 1990s saw a fairly stable Jerry Garcia Band lineup, featuring keyboardist Seals, bassist Kahn, vocalists Gloria Jones and Jackie LaBranch, and drummer David Kemper. The Jerry Garcia Band delighted fans when the Dead weren't touring and played many of the same venues. In the 1980s Garcia also played with the Jerry Garcia Acoustic Band, which would often open for the Jerry Garcia Band. Since Garcia's death in 1995, the Garcia family estate has released live recordings from all of his various non-Grateful Dead bands. Who knows what exceptional gems may be forthcoming?

Weir: The Band Leader

Bob Weir's non-Dead career was slow to start. Technically, *Ace* from 1972 is a Weir solo album, but all the members of the Grateful Dead played on it. *Ace* features fine studio renditions of Grateful Dead classics like "Playing in the Band" and new songs like the bluesy "Black Throated Wind." It was the first album to feature Weir's longstanding songwriting partner, John Perry Barlow.

The Dead's mid-'70s hiatus jumpstarted Weir's non-Dead discography. He joined rock 'n' blues outfit Kingfish in 1974. In addition to touring with the band, he contributed to a studio album in 1976 and a live album in 1977. When

Bob Weir jams with The Other Ones in September 2000.

THE SCRANTON TIMES/BUTCH COMEGYS/AP PHOTO

ALBUM SPOTLIGHT

Bobby and the Midnites, *Where the Beat Meets the Street*

Despite the fact that Bob Weir now says he wishes this album would go away, it deserves some reevaluation. Yes, this album was an attempt to try and get the Midnites some top 40 success, and it may be true that the other Midnite members were trying to lure Weir away from the Grateful Dead during this period. It's filled with 1980s-sounding pop songs with slick production from Jeff Baxter, and it spawned an embarrassing MTV video for "I Want to Live in America." All that said, there is nothing wrong with good pop songs, and the songs here are very good, with the Weir/Barlow tune "Gloria Monday" a classic. While definitely and defiantly not the Grateful Dead, this album deserves a listen.

Bob Weir performs with his band Rat-Dog, which he formed just before Jerry Garcia died in 1995.

SUSANA MILLMAN

Bobby Ace and the Cards from the Bottom of the Deck

Bobby Ace and the Cards from the Bottom of the Deck was an offshoot band that remains a Dead mystery. Bobby Ace only played a few shows, none of which have yet been found on any recordings. The lineup at a show in '69 included most of the members of the Grateful Dead plus two players from New Riders of the Purple Sage. The lineup at a handful of shows in 1970 was (probably) a stripped-down version of the Dead.

the Dead resumed touring, Weir left Kingfish but soon released a solo album. Working with producer Keith Olson, who had produced the Dead's 1977 *Terrapin Station*, Weir recorded *Heaven Help the Fool* in 1978. It was overproduced — a recurring fault in Weir's work — but had some good songs, like "Heaven Help the Fool," "Shade of Grey" and a cover of Little Feat's "Easy to Slip."

After his solo album, Weir formed Bobby and the Midnites, a band that toured in the early 1980s and released albums in 1981 and 1984. Live, Bobby and the Midnites were fantastic, featuring the amazing drum skills of jazz-fusionist Billy Cobham. After Bobby and the Midnites faded, Weir toured with bassist Rob Wasserman in the late 1980s and the two performed as an acoustic duo in the early 1990s before releasing *Weir and Wasserman Live* in 1998. Weir formed

Bob Weir (right) and Phil Lesh play with Grateful Dead successor band The Other Ones.

DARREN HAUCK/AP PHOTO

rockers RatDog in 1995, just before Garcia died. RatDog's musical repertoire features Grateful Dead songs, covers and originals. RatDog released its sole studio album, *Evening Moods,* in 2000.

Lesh: A Late Bloomer

During the three decades Phil Lesh was in the Grateful Dead, he only occasionally played outside the band. Along with several other members of the Dead, Lesh played on David Crosby's well-received 1971 album *If I Could Only Remember My Name,* as well as several albums by Graham Nash and David Bromberg. He played in the short-lived Too Loose Ta Truck with guitarist Terry Haggerty (a member of Sons of Champlin) for a brief period in 1976, and played several gigs with the Jerry Garcia

ALBUM SPOTLIGHT

Seastones

During the Grateful Dead's 1974 tours, Phil Lesh was joined by electronic musician Ned Lagin between the first and second sets for a series of musical experiments. Lagin released a studio album, *Seastones,* on Round Records in 1975. Many members of the Dead contributed to the album, including Lesh, and it was pushed as a Lesh album at the time. It's not a collection of songs, but rather electronic sounds, voices and noises. The album has been cited as a great influence on today's industrial, electronic and techno musicians. If you had to put it into a musical category, you might call it a minimalist musique concrète art symphony. It's a fascinating listen if you have big enough ears to enjoy it!

Band in 1981. In the '80s Lesh worked on a symphony called "Noosphere," and in 1994, his dream of conducting a symphony was realized when he was a guest conductor for a benefit concert of the Berkeley Symphony Orchestra.

With the demise of the Grateful Dead, Lesh, perhaps surprisingly, became a very active bandleader. Starting in 1999, Lesh put his energies into Phil Lesh & Friends. Lesh's concept for the band was to have an ever-changing group of musicians play with him. Some of those who have been in the band include Steve Kimock, the Black Crowes' Chris Robinson, John Scofield, Jackie Brown, John Mediski, the Allman Brother's Warren Hayes, Joan Osborne and Lesh's own children Brian and Grahame. In 2002, Phil Lesh & Friends released its only studio album, *There and Back Again*. Featuring straight-ahead rock 'n' roll, it highlights Lesh's vocal abilities.

Right: Though never a member of the Grateful Dead, Jimmy Herring has played with both Phil Lesh and Friends and the Dead.

Bottom: Bob Weir (left) and Phil Lesh helped keep the spirit of the Grateful Dead alive while performing with The Other Ones.

TOP: WIKI COMMONS, BOTTOM: SUSANA MILLMAN